Mere
Discipleship

Mere Discipleship

Growing in Wisdom and Hope

ALISTER E. McGRATH

BakerBooks
a division of Baker Publishing Group
Grand Rapids, Michigan

Originally published by Society for Promoting Christian Knowledge

Published in North America by Baker Books
a division of Baker Publishing Group
PO Box 6287, Grand Rapids, MI 49516-6287
www.bakerbooks.com

Printed in the United States of America

Library of Congress Cataloging-in-Publication Data
Names: McGrath, Alister E., 1953– author.
Title: Mere discipleship : Growing in wisdom and hope / Alister McGrath.
Description: Grand Rapids, MI : Baker Books, a division of Baker Publishing Group, [2019]
    | "First published in Great Britain in 2018, Society for Promoting Christian Knowledge." |
    Includes bibliographical references andindex.
Identifiers: LCCN 2018034283| ISBN 9780801094224 (paperback : alk. paper) | ISBN
    9781493417513 (ebook)
Subjects: LCSH: Spiritual formation. | Christian life.
Classification: LCC BV4501.3 .M3395 2019 | DDC 248.4—dc23
LC record available at https://lccn.loc.gov/2018034283

19 20 21 22 23 24 25   7 6 5 4 3 2 1

To Regent College,
Vancouver

Contents

Contents

Part 3 Journeying in Hope: Four Sermons

Introduction

We are drowning in information, while starving for wisdom.
Edward O. Wilson[1]

This short book deals with the theme of Christian discipleship—the quest to go beyond a superficial grasp of our faith, discover its depths and riches, and be refreshed and transformed by them. "Discipleship" is not a biblical term; it is, however, most certainly a biblical theme. It is about a conscious and committed decision to be followers of Jesus Christ in every way possible, including the way we think, love, and act. It is about growing in our faith, as we quest for wisdom rather than the mere accumulation of information about Christianity. Discipleship is rooted in a secure, reflective, and deepening grasp of the Christian gospel. This kind of wisdom goes far beyond a simple (and often superficial) knowledge of basic Christian ideas. It arises from a deep and prolonged personal reflection on the Christian faith over an extended period of time, informing both thought and action.

This quest for Christian wisdom lies at the heart of a "discipleship of the mind"—an acquired habit of understanding and imagining ourselves and our world that is firmly rooted in the Christian gospel.

It allows us to see things as they really are, stripping away illusions and misunderstandings. It also helps us with what the American philosopher John Dewey called the "deepest problem of modern life"—that we have failed to integrate our "thoughts about the world" with our thoughts about "value and purpose."[2] We don't just want to know how things *work*; we want to know what they *mean*.

Yet the discipleship of the mind does not take the form of an immediate illumination of our minds, as if there is some dramatic moment of clarification through which we suddenly find ourselves in possession of full answers to all of life's questions. Rather, it is a process of gradual growth in wisdom, paralleling an athlete's training regime, through which we absorb and assimilate the Christian vision of reality and allow it to percolate through our minds and inform the way in which we think, imagine, and act. Happily, other people can help us do this—especially those who have thought about this over many years. This is one reason why engaging with writers who are thought to be wise—such as the four figures considered in the second part of this work—can be so helpful.

As in my earlier work *Mere Theology* (2010),[3] I engage regularly and appreciatively with C. S. Lewis, now widely regarded as one of the most significant Christian writers of the twentieth century.[4] I draw on Lewis in two ways. First, I endorse Lewis's notion of a generous consensual Christian orthodoxy, famously set out in his classic work *Mere Christianity* (1952). This emphasizes the core ideas that Christians share in common, without advocating any specific denominational agenda. Christian discipleship transcends denominational boundaries, even though it can be enriched by the spiritual traditions of individual denominations.

Second, I frequently use Lewis himself as a point of reference in this work, not least on account of his idea of Christianity as offering a "big picture" of reality, which helps us to see ourselves and our world in a new way. This basic theme is expressed with particular clarity in an image used by Lewis in the concluding sentence of his landmark lecture "Is Theology Poetry?" (1945), which is explicitly referenced at three points in this work and implicitly assumed at many others: "I believe in Christianity as I believe that the Sun has risen, not only because I see it, but because by it I see everything else."[5] For Lewis, the "big picture" that lies at the heart of the Christian faith allows us to discern the patterns of meaning and value that lie behind and beneath our observations. Discipleship is about grasping this picture and living meaningfully within its frame.

Each of the thirteen chapters gathered together in this collection addresses aspects of the theme of discipleship. Some had their origins as sermons, some as informal talks, and some as major public presentations over the period 2010–17. I have edited these lectures and presentations to reduce their size, achieve consistency of style, and sharpen their focus.

The work is divided into three parts. The first consists of five substantial chapters introducing the discipleship of the mind, developing the general theme of what I like to call the "reflective inhabitation" of the Christian faith. To be a Christian is not to passively accept a set of intellectual beliefs, but to take delight in them and explore their implications for the ways in which we think and behave. As the Spanish philosopher José Ortega y Gasset observed, we exist within a world that is shaped and nourished by beliefs,[6] which in turn shape our mental and spiritual life. These beliefs shape our vision of reality: "In them we live, move, and exist."[7] They concern what really matters and the difference that this makes to the business of life.

Ludwig Wittgenstein made a similar point, suggesting that religious belief is about "passionately taking up" an interpretation of the world, so that it is not simply a way of thinking but "a way of living."[8] Good theology is thus about fostering authentic and meaningful living, not simply right thinking. And for Christians, that life of faith is supported and nourished by the community of faith—by the church.[9]

Christians stand within and belong to a community of reflection and proclamation, deeply rooted in the past yet able and willing to engage the issues of the present. We gain insights and wisdom from those who have journeyed in faith before us, as well as those who are now journeying alongside us on the road. These five chapters open up and explore some important themes, such as how the creeds help us deepen our faith, the role of the church in encouraging discipleship, and the place of books and mentors in our personal growth.

The second part of this work is more focused, looking at four leading recent exemplars of a discipleship of the mind—Dorothy L. Sayers (1893–1957), C. S. Lewis (1898–1963), John Stott (1921–2011), and J. I. Packer (born 1926). These chapters were originally public lectures. These four writers have developed their own distinct modes of reflective inhabitation of the Christian faith from which there is much to be learned. These are only four of the writers who have become my fellow wayfarers on the road of faith. It goes without saying that many others—such as Marilynne Robinson—could easily have been included. I have highlighted some points made by these four that I personally find both wise and illuminating. Most of us end up adopting a group of writers as our trusted friends—not because we agree with them on everything, but because we find them to be thoughtful, engaging, and helpful. Even when we disagree with them on some things, we find others that they help us find new insights into.

Finally, the third part of this work brings together four sermons touching on the discipleship of the mind, focusing on how we cope with journeying in hope through darkness. The elusive word "hope" has been the subject of immense interest in recent years. Dozens of theories and definitions have been put forward about what the word means, and the difference that hope makes to human life.[10] Christianity has always known this idea, which it sees in its own distinctive way as allowing us to cope with suffering, to journey through darkness, and to live meaningfully in a world in which things often don't seem to make complete sense. The Christian philosopher John Macmurray captures this aspect of hope well: "The maxim of illusory religion runs: 'Fear not; trust in God and he will see that none of the things you fear will happen to you'; that of real religion, on the contrary is, 'Fear not; the things that you are afraid of are quite likely to happen to you, but they are nothing to be afraid of.'"[11]

Two of these final four pieces are university sermons, one preached before the University of Oxford in 2016, the other before the University of Cambridge in 2015. These sermons are traditionally seen as substantial reflections on aspects of the Christian faith, intended to engage and stimulate university audiences. The remaining two are much shorter, representing sermons preached in Oxford in 2013 and 2014, which were broadcast live on BBC Radio 4. As the BBC allowed me only 1,000 words for these sermons, I found myself struggling to pack as much insight as possible into such a short piece.

It remains for me to thank those who invited me to give these lectures and presentations in the first place, and my many correspondents who urged me to publish them in the second. There is much more that needs to be said about all the themes engaged in this collection, yet I hope these pieces will serve as useful starting points for going "further up and further in" (C. S. Lewis) to the life of faith.

I have pleasure in dedicating this small volume to Regent College, Vancouver, a school of theology that excels in bringing together heart and mind in exploring and grasping the riches of the Christian faith. I have long valued my association with this school and its dedicated and talented faculty.

Alister E. McGrath
Oxford

PART 1

The Discipleship of the Mind

Five Reflections

1

The Lord Is My Light

On the Discipleship of the Mind

The LORD is my light and my salvation; whom shall I fear?

Psalm 27:1

These opening words of Psalm 27 are familiar to us all. For me, they have a special significance, given my long association with Oxford University, as its motto is *Dominus illuminatio mea*, "The Lord is my light." My topic in this chapter is the rich and exciting idea that the Christian faith opens up new ways of thinking and has the potential to have an impact on the church, the academy, and society as a whole.[1] I want to commend a "discipleship of the mind," in which we deliberately and intentionally cultivate a Christian habit of thought, as part of the grace-wrought process of transformation by the gospel.

This chapter is based on the 2010 Laing Lecture, delivered at the London School of Theology on February 23, 2010.

The Christian faith helps us to form habits of seeing and shape directions of gaze that change the way in which we think about things, experience the world, and act within it. It gives us a new way of perceiving the world,[2] allowing us to understand ourselves and this world in a distinctively Christian way. We acquire a new way of thinking, which differs radically from the habits of thought we pick up from the natural world and from secular culture. We need to be helped to see things as they really are; the "natural" human perspective on things needs to be transformed by divine grace. In this chapter, I shall explore some ways in which the Christian faith illuminates reality, as a way of encouraging both a discipleship of the mind and a committed and informed engagement with our culture.

Light has long been seen as an important analogy for truth.[3] In speaking about God as our light, we are speaking of both the human capacity to see and God's ability to illuminate. The two are interconnected: without light, we cannot see; the effectiveness of a source of light is judged by what it enables us to see and how well it allows us to find our way through the darkness. The renewal of our minds and the reshaping of its habits are part of the transformation and renewal that are brought by the gospel (Rom. 12:2).

The Shaping of a Christian Mind

It is more than half a century since Harry Blamires (1916–2017) published his landmark work *The Christian Mind*.[4] Blamires's work was clearly inspired by C. S. Lewis, who was one of the formative influences in persuading him to write it. *The Christian Mind* opens by documenting the "lack of a Christian mind," before moving on to set out a programmatic vision of how such a mind could be recovered.

Blamires noted that most of the books that shaped and molded culture in his day were being written by non-Christians. He called for a renewal of a Christian life of the mind, especially in the academy and professions. It is far from clear that things have improved since then. I very much fear that Christianity is in danger of becoming detached from public debates and discussions—not because of any failings with the Christian vision of reality but due to a lack of vision and confidence on the part of some of its leaders and representatives.

I believe that the situation faced by Christianity throughout the West makes the renewal of the Christian mind imperative. The rise of the "New Atheism"—a rhetorically aggressive movement associated especially with Richard Dawkins and Christopher Hitchens—has seen fundamental challenges to the rationality of the Christian faith that are more than capable of being countered, if (and it is a big "if") Christians know enough about their faith and are willing to affirm and defend its core themes in the public domain.

We need to develop a discipleship of the mind that will help Christians appreciate the rational and existential strengths of their faith, as well as the corresponding weaknesses of the New Atheism. There are three basic criticisms that can be made of the New Atheism, to which others could easily be added.[5]

1. The New Atheism criticizes concepts of God that bear little relation to those associated with Christianity. It ridicules caricatures and parodies of Christianity rather than engaging respectfully with authentic Christian ideas and practices.
2. It offers hopelessly oversimplified accounts of religion—such as the discredited but still influential Victorian notion that science and religion are necessarily and permanently at war with each other—without indicating that these views are no longer taken seriously by academic scholarship.
3. It demands that religious people "prove" their ideas, while failing to apply these same criteria of judgment to its own beliefs.

This third point is particularly important, given the New Atheism's persistent and uncritical suggestion that "faith" is invariably "blind faith." The philosopher Bertrand Russell is often described as an "atheist" in popular secularist publications. In fact, Russell was far too sophisticated a thinker to allow himself to be categorized in this way. Rather, like the earlier philosopher David Hume, Russell maintained a skeptical attitude to metaphysical questions. Philosophy teaches us how to cope with such uncertainty, Russell suggested— including uncertainty about whether there is, or is not, a God. "To teach how to live without certainty, and yet without being paralysed by hesitation, is perhaps the chief thing that philosophy, in our age, can still do for those who study it."[6] Epistemologically, Russell was an agnostic, who knew he could not prove atheism was right; he therefore, in effect, chose to live as an atheist, realizing that this attitude (like its religious counterpart) lay beyond final verification.[7]

When all is said and done, the New Atheism is a rhetorically supercharged agnosticism that hopes the ferocity of its words will divert attention from the poverty of its arguments. Everyone, whether religious or secular, ends up believing some things—often some very important things—that they cannot *prove* to be true. That's just the dilemma we face as human beings.

My point here is that Christians need to gain confidence in their own ideas if they are to offer a plausible rebuttal of the New Atheist worldview. To appreciate the importance of this point, we might reflect on some words of the Oxford theologian and New Testament scholar Austin Farrer. Writing shortly after the death of C. S. Lewis, Farrer tried to pinpoint the grounds of Lewis's remarkable and continuing success as a cultural apologist. In part, Farrer believed that this was due to Lewis's ability to demonstrate the reasonableness of faith: "Though argument does not create conviction, the lack of it destroys belief. What seems to be proved may not be embraced; but what no one shows the ability to defend is quickly abandoned. Rational argument does not create belief, but it maintains a climate in which belief may flourish."[8] Farrer is surely right. Responding to intellectual and cultural criticisms of faith may not lead to conversion and conviction. Yet a failure to respond creates the impression that faith is for those who have neither the ability nor inclination to think, that faith lacks any evidential basis, or that the death of faith is the inevitable outcome of cultural progress. The lack of a plausible and informed rejoinder to these criticisms merely solidifies the growing impression in Western culture at large that Christian faith is an endangered species that belongs to a less critical prescientific age.

Anti-Intellectualism and the "Foolishness" of the Gospel

As a close observer of the Christian scene in the West, I am disturbed at the recent rise of anti-intellectualism and a lack of interest in scholarship within many churches, encouraged by some Christian leaders. I happened to be present at a meeting of some evangelical students some years ago, when Richard Dawkins's *God Delusion* was being discussed. The basic consensus was that there was no need to take Dawkins's arguments seriously or set out a Christian alternative. The solution that their leader recommended was an energetic and frequent public citation of Psalm 14:1: "Fools say in their hearts, 'There is no God.'" I intend no disrespect here but this rather smug response is totally unacceptable. It represents a lack of vision, a loss of nerve and, above all, a failure to take the gospel seriously and give good answers when the situation demands it (1 Pet. 3:15).[9]

One of the great themes of the rich Christian vision of reality is that it has the power to attract and convict morally, imaginatively, and rationally. Grasping the truth of this vision inexorably leads on to the appreciation of its delight, wonder, excitement, and challenge. Christian leaders are called on to act as channels, mediums, or conduits for the glory of the Christian vision, allowing it to have an impact on our culture, using images and words that this culture can understand. A recovery of the life of the mind is essential for the survival and well-being of the church.

My concern in this chapter is to reaffirm the need to love God with "all [our] mind" (Mark 12:29–30) as an integral aspect of the Christian life of faith. Not only is this mandated by the gospel; it enables us to go deeper into our faith and engage with those outside the church who have questions, doubts, or objections about the Christian faith. Every faculty we possess is to be placed at the service of the gospel. Paul urges his readers to be transformed through the renewing of their minds that the gospel brings about (Rom. 12:2). It is essential that this process of intellectual renewal and redirection is encouraged and the shape of a Christian mind is explored.

Some Christians resist Paul's injunctions for the renewal of the mind, arguing that he elsewhere asserts that Christianity represents a form of "foolishness" opposed to human knowledge and wisdom (such as 1 Cor. 1:18). Yet this represents a misreading of Paul's concerns about the situation at Corinth on the one hand and what is meant by the notion of a "Christian mind" on the other. Paul believed that the church at Corinth was in danger of being influenced by early forms of Gnosticism, which held that individuals were saved by a secret, arcane knowledge, known only to a few privileged insiders. Others at Corinth prized intellectual sophistication and were not prepared to tolerate anything that seemed to lack this or other marks of cultural erudition.[10] Paul rightly rejects any such notions, insisting that the Christian gospel must be taken on its own terms, even if it counters prevailing cultural notions of acceptability or wisdom.

Paul declares that Christians possess "the mind of Christ" (1 Cor. 2:16), which he distinguishes from alternative approaches to wisdom already present at Corinth. A "Christian mind" is the distinctive mind-set, a way of thinking that is shaped and nourished by the Christian faith.[11] It is not about a quest for exotic or arcane knowledge, or the cultivation of academic arrogance; rather, it is about allowing the light of Christ to shine on our intellects, so that the transforming power of God's grace might renew our minds, not merely our souls. Christianity is shaped by a rich and coherent trinitarian logic of faith, which calls into question the thinner rationalities of secular culture and offers a more satisfying view of the world.[12]

The Gospel and the Illumination of Reality

Let me return to the image with which I opened this chapter—God as a source of light, illuminating the realities of human existence and the natural order, and showing them up for what they really are. It has become familiar to many through the writings of C. S. Lewis, which regularly explore the idea of God as a sun or a source of light that allows us to see things properly. The Christian idea of God, for Lewis, is both intelligible and the source of intelligibility—a theme summed up in his signature declaration, "I believe in Christianity as I believe that the Sun has risen, not only because I see it, but because by it I see everything else."[13] The clarity of intellectual and spiritual vision offered by the Christian faith is thus itself, in Lewis's mind, an indicator of its truth. I regularly make use of this landmark statement, which is both imaginatively engaging and intellectually illuminating.

Let us pause here and make sure that we have understood what Lewis is saying through this visually striking analogy. Lewis suggests that the process of observation involves two elements: the human act of seeing and the process of illumination, which allows things to be seen. There are limits to human vision, as we all know when we try to make out the features of a landscape on a moonless night or find our way around a dark cellar. Lewis's first point is that the gospel illuminates the world, so our natural human limitations are transcended. It is a theme familiar to any reader of Scripture: "Your word is a lamp to my feet and a light to my path" (Ps. 119:105). As Augustine of Hippo once remarked, "The mind needs to be enlightened by light from outside itself, so that it can participate in truth, as it is not itself the nature of truth. You will light my lamp, Lord."[14] We must not overinterpret Augustine's imagery here; the point he is making is that God, as the source of all truth, graciously helps humanity to find that truth. Without that help, there are limits to what we can discover.[15]

The second theme that is implicit in Lewis's image is the importance of the human act of seeing. While some philosophers of the Enlightenment era used to treat seeing as a passive process in which we merely absorb information from our environment, it is now recognized to be an active process, in which we put together the elements of our picture of the world. We can be trained to see more effectively, by learning what we should be looking for. We can cultivate habits of heightened attention and perception, which make us more alert to what is present around us—things that otherwise we might look at but not notice or appreciate.

Part of the process of Christian discipleship is the cultivation of theological attentiveness, which helps us to deliberately see things from the perspective of faith and savor what we find. The American novelist Henry Miller captured this point well when he noted that "the moment one gives close attention to any thing, even a blade of grass, it becomes a mysterious, awesome, indescribably magnificent world in itself."[16] Christ's command to "consider the lilies of the field" (Matt. 6:28–29) is an excellent example of the outcome of such attentiveness, paralleled in some ways by Geoffrey Chaucer's "Ode to a Daisy."[17] More recently, Gerard Manley Hopkins's poem "God's Grandeur" models a theologically principled and spiritually fruitful attentiveness to the created order, arising from a disciplined Christian engagement with the world of nature.[18]

This way of thinking and seeing is a habit of mind, something that is to be practiced and cultivated. It is nourished by reading Scripture and inhabiting the worship-shaped world of the church, in which the Christian story is constantly presented and represented. Yet this is not something that we merely absorb passively; we must actively develop it, deliberately and consciously asking how we might deepen our understanding of our faith. This is what I hope we might find—but fear that we all too often do not find—in Christian preaching.

Christianity gives us a new set of spectacles through which we see the world, allowing us to discern its deeper logic. The world is illuminated by the light of the gospel and interpreted by the believing mind. This process of "seeing" involves both intellectual analysis and value judgments. It is not a set of principles that are learned by heart and regurgitated on demand. Rather, it is an acquired mode of reflection, a habit of thinking, that is both commended and embodied in the Christian story.

The Christian faith enables us to see the world in a manner that transcends the empirical. It offers us theoretical spectacles that allow us to behold things in such a way that we are able to rise above the limits of the observable and move into the richer realm of discerned meaning and value. The natural world thus becomes seen and interpreted as God's creation, bearing the subtle imprint of its maker. We see not only the empirical reality of the world but also its deeper value and true significance. Neither value nor significance, it must be emphasized, are empirical notions—things that we can see around us. They must be discerned and then superimposed on an empirical reading of the world.

The Discipleship of the Mind and Christian Witness

We are called to exercise a Christian discipleship of the mind in every area of life. Whether we are called to serve God in the arts or in music, in health work or in international development, in the academy or in politics, we must work out what it means to be a Christian in these contexts. Sometimes this will mean manifesting and embodying the love, compassion, and care that is so central a feature of the life of faith. Sometimes it will involve challenging ideologies that have become deeply embedded in the academy, culture, or society. There is no area of life in which we are excused by God from the need to work out our discipleship. We are called to be witnesses, to allow our light to be seen; to be salt to the world around us. And we can only do that through our presence in the world—through inhabiting situations to which we feel called.

Some Christians withdraw from society, believing that it contaminates the purity of their faith and morals. Yet to refuse to inhabit or engage society is to deny God the opportunity to use us as a channel and conduit for the presence of Christ. We are called to be in the world but not of the world—in other words, to be present and available in secular society but not to conform to its ideologies, ethos, and ideas. The Christian challenge is thus to reflect on how we might transform the world rather than conform to it. Yet we can only transform our world by inhabiting it, learning its language, and telling it about the "boundless riches of Christ" (Eph. 3:8).

So where do we need to be, if this is to happen? Whether this question is posed geographically or sociologically, the answer is the same: *everywhere*. For the purposes of this chapter, however, I want to emphasize particularly the importance of engaging with the academy and the learned professions. Whether we speak of poets, economists, lawyers, bankers, or philosophers, the issue for Christian discipleship remains essentially the same: a quest for professional competence that is both energized and informed by the Christian vision of reality. The first question that might be asked is, How can your faith make you a better lawyer? The second might be, How can your faith make the law better? How does the "mind of Christ" bear on this specific professional community?

We have now come to a point where specificity begins to become important. It is one thing to outline a general principle, but how is it to be put into practice? I must now turn to the question of how faith interacts with professional lives. It is clearly beyond the scope of this chapter to look at a wide range of professional activities. In his *Christian Mind*, Harry Blamires examined how the life of the mind could be explored in a number of academic disciplines. You will have to forgive me for restricting myself here to one area of professional activity in which I myself engaged for several years—the study of the natural sciences. I want to use this as an example of the kind of thinking and reflection that needs to be done. So what insights and motivations does the Christian faith bring to this area of activity?

A Case Study: The Natural Sciences

My own time as a scientist impressed on me the privilege of being able to investigate a universe that is both rationally transparent and rationally beautiful, capable of being represented in elegant mathematical forms. One of the most significant parallels between the natural sciences and Christian theology is a fundamental conviction that the world is characterized by regularity and intelligibility.[19] The natural sciences are founded on the perception of an explicable regularity to the world, which is capable of being represented mathematically. In other words, there is something about the world—and the nature of the human mind—that allows patterns within nature to be discerned and represented.

This perception of ordering and intelligibility is of immense significance, at both the scientific and religious levels. As Paul Davies points out, "In Renaissance Europe, the justification for what we today call the scientific approach to inquiry was the belief in a rational God whose created order could be discerned from a careful study of nature."[20] Yet how are we to account for the regularity of nature? And for the human ability to represent it so well? Where do our notions of explanation, regularity, and intelligibility come from? Why is nature actually intelligible to us? The human capacity for understanding our world seems to be far in excess of anything that could reasonably be considered to be simply an evolutionary necessity or even a fortuitous by-product of the evolutionary process. As Albert Einstein observed, "The most incomprehensible thing about the universe is that it is comprehensible."[21] Einstein rightly saw that the question of the intelligibility of our universe might be raised by science but cannot be answered by science.

The physicist-turned-theologian John Polkinghorne is one of many who have highlighted the importance of the "congruence between our minds and the universe, between the rationality experienced within and the rationality observed without."[22] A naturalistic metaphysics, he suggests, is unable to cast light on the deep intelligibility of the universe. A theistic metaphysics argues, however, that there is a common origin to both the rationality that we experience within our minds and the rational structure we observe in the physical world around us. Both are grounded in the rationality of God. In other words, Christianity offers an intellectual framework, a way of understanding and seeing our world, that makes sense of what is otherwise little more than a happy coincidence or an inexplicable (though fortunate) cosmic accident.

Others have pointed to the growing interest in anthropic phenomena and suggested that these are also consonant with a Christian way of thinking.[23] The heavily freighted vocabulary of "fine-tuning" is widely used to express the idea that the universe appears to have possessed certain qualities from the moment of its inception that were favorable to the production of intelligent life on Earth at this point in cosmic history, capable of reflecting on the implications of its existence.[24] As I point out in my 2009 Gifford Lectures at the ancient University of Aberdeen, these themes resonate strongly with the Christian vision of reality.[25] They prove nothing, and other explanations are certainly possible, yet there is an intellectual resonance that can hardly be ignored. The Christian mental map makes sense of this aspect of the natural world, as it does of so much of the scientific enterprise as a whole. Yet it does more than just make sense of things; it offers us a critical framework within which we can operate professionally. Let me explain what I mean by this.

Science is an activity that is carried out by human beings. So what understanding of human nature undergirds this enterprise and informs its outcomes? The Enlightenment had a thoroughly optimistic view of human nature; we are good people, who want to do good things. Science thus enables us to build a better world. Yet few would now share this charmingly innocent and naive view of human nature. The wars of the twentieth century have put an end to such naivety, not least because of the widespread application of science to the development of weapons of mass destruction.

The history of the twentieth century is perhaps the greatest obstacle that the metanarrative of secular progress has to overcome, especially in relation to its core assumption of the fundamental goodness of humanity. The First World War, the Great Depression, and the Second World War all raised awkward questions about the plausibility of this narrative. We were told that if we got rid of religion—or at least neutralized it, pulling out its teeth—then the likelihood of war would be drastically reduced, since religion was a key element in causing global conflict. Yet as far as scholars can see, there were no significant religious motivations for either the First World War (death toll around 16 million) or the Second World War (death toll around 60 million).

The cultural critic Terry Eagleton ridiculed the Enlightenment dream of "untrammelled human progress" as a "bright-eyed superstition," a fairy tale that lacks any rigorous evidential base. "If ever there was a pious myth and a piece of credulous superstition, it is the liberal-rationalist belief that, a few hiccups apart, we are all steadily *en route* to a finer world."[26] Science has become woven into this rationalist myth, and it is time to challenge this naive account of history. We are invited to question fictions about both human individuals and society, even if these consoling fictions are deeply embedded within the secular Western mind-set.

Richard Dawkins and other writers associated with the New Atheism often accuse those who believe in God of holding on to "unevidenced beliefs," in contrast to the rigorously proven factual statements of their own enlightened atheism. Yet what of its own unevidenced and uncritical belief in human progress? Eagleton dismisses this myth as a demonstrably false pastiche, a luminous example of "blind faith."[27] What rational soul, Eagleton asks, would sign up to such a secular myth, which is obliged to treat such human-created catastrophes as Hiroshima, Auschwitz, and apartheid as "a few local hiccups" that in no way discredit or disrupt the steady upward progress of history?

My concern here is not to debate the ethics of napalm or nuclear weapons, but to emphasize the need for a critical perspective that avoids any idealization of human history or any specific area of professional life, such as the natural sciences. A realistic view of human nature is essential if we are to make sense of the failures and foibles evident in the worlds of politics, business, science, and economics and do something about them.

Conclusion

In this chapter, I have concentrated on an area I know well—the natural sciences—but the approach to discipleship that I have briefly outlined here can be applied to other professional contexts and academic disciplines. We need individuals who are both theologically informed and professionally competent, who can make the connections between these two domains. Professional competence is now a precondition for professional attention. For Christianity to be taken seriously in this important area of life, we need committed and competent people who can model professional excellence and personal commitment. They need to see this for what it really is—a *vocation*, something to which God calls us that is different from but no less important than ordained ministry.

So why is this important? Let me mention just two points here in closing. The first point is so obvious that I hesitate to develop it. We need competent Christians to be salt and light in the professions and the academic world. We cannot allow a Christian presence to be excluded from any area of our culture. Some are trying to exclude a Christian voice as part of their secularizing agenda or in pursuit of a misguided interpretation of the idea of "multiculturalism" that affirms every cultural option except Christianity. These need to be challenged, but I am concerned about something much more disturbing—the failure of the churches to articulate a "theology of calling" that values and, above all, encourages Christians to enter professional sectors and see themselves as having a ministry there.

Second, as I have just noted, many areas of professional and academic life have come to be shaped by ideologies that often have quite strongly antireligious tones. As an example of this, we might note the curiously uncontested discursive privilege accorded by many social theorists to atheism. The most obvious explanation of this otherwise puzzling phenomenon is that atheism has successfully presented itself as the "rational default category" against which all other beliefs are to be judged. Atheism is held to offer a neutral standpoint, a position of "value neutrality," that allows religious beliefs and behaviors to be examined and assessed without the distorting influence of faith commitments.[28] This is simply not the case, yet it can easily become the accepted wisdom of our age if Christians fail to challenge it and demonstrate that there are better readings of this situation.

I have set out a vision of the "mind of Christ" as an acquired habit of mind, a mental discipline, that transforms the way in which we see the world and ourselves, and thus inspires us to reflective and informed action. I have emphasized the intellectual capaciousness and resilience of the Christian faith, which enables it to engage meaningfully with the contemporary cultural concerns. Yet I have also raised concerns about the failure of the churches to articulate a "theology of calling" that recognizes that God equips and calls people to be his servants and witnesses in every corner of life— including the professional and academic worlds.

The New Atheism has issued a wake-up call to the churches. We need a new generation of public intellectuals who will value the life of the mind and realize its importance for apologetics and evangelism. Yes, there is more to the gospel than its new vision of reality, but we need to make sure that vision is powerfully and faithfully proclaimed. There is no need to make Christianity relevant or to make it credible. It already possesses these attributes, which are deeply embedded within its inner logic. Our task is to discover and appreciate the intellectual depths and delights of our faith and ensure that these are proclaimed and presented to our culture at large. It helps us in our own journey of faith, as we aim to grow in wisdom; yet perhaps more importantly, it deepens the quality and power of our witness to God as our light and our salvation to those around us.

2

Belief

The Place of the Creeds in the Life of Faith

In this chapter, I shall reflect on the place of the creeds in the life of faith. It is a wonderful theme, allowing me to open up the way in which these summaries of faith can help us with the business of Christian discipleship.[1] It is a topic that many have addressed before me, including John Pearson, bishop of Chester from 1673 to 1686, who was the author of the classic *Exposition of the Creed* (1659). Pearson was a learned establishment figure of the Restoration era, who was successively Lady Margaret Professor of Divinity at Cambridge University; master of Trinity College, Cambridge; and finally bishop of Chester. He served as chaplain to Charles II and was elected a Fellow of the Royal Society in 1667. His *Exposition of the Creed*, often cited as a model of classical Anglican divinity, exercised a calming influence during a period of theological turbulence and helped to shape the religious consensus that emerged within England in the late seventeenth and early

This chapter is based on a lecture given to the Chester Theological Society in Chester Cathedral on May 11, 2011.

eighteenth centuries. The great essayist Samuel Johnson (1709–84) spoke highly of Pearson's work and commended it as a model of persuasive, generous orthodoxy.

Yet my topic here is not Pearson's *Exposition of the Creed* itself. Instead, I shall use it as a point of departure for a discussion of the place of creeds in the Christian life, and especially the discipleship of the mind. As Pearson rightly saw, the purpose of creeds was to offer the following benefits:

1. A public, authorized statement of faith rather than the private perception of an individual. They set out the shared faith of the church, not that of any one individual.
2. A framework for making sense of the world and our own inner life. While Pearson tends to focus on the outward aspects of faith, the Wesleyan revivals of the early eighteenth century led others to develop its inner aspects.
3. A guidebook to the key themes of faith, which is not intended to be a substitute for detailed exploration of its depths—any more than the rather brief entry on "Chester" in the *Lonely Planet Great Britain* guide is a substitute for an extended visit there.

Let's set the scene for our discussion. In 1930, the celebrity author Evelyn Waugh (1903–66)—whose novel *Vile Bodies* had been hailed earlier that year as "*the* ultramodern novel"—dropped a bombshell in literary circles by announcing that he had been received into the Catholic Church. The development was so unexpected and significant that it immediately made the front pages of one of Britain's leading newspapers, the *Daily Express*. How, its editor wondered, could an author best known for his "almost passionate adherence to the ultramodern" have embraced the Christian faith? For the next week, the paper's columns were filled with comment and reflection on this seemingly baffling development.

Waugh spoke of his delight in discovering this new way of engaging reality in a letter he wrote to his friend Edward Sackville-West in 1949: "Conversion is like stepping across the chimney piece out of a Looking-Glass world, where everything is an absurd caricature, into the real world God made; and then begins the delicious process of exploring it limitlessly."[2] There are two points that Waugh makes here, and both are highly relevant to my theme. First, faith removes distortions; it lets us see things as they really are. The New Testament uses a wide range of images, such as illumination or the removal of an obscuring veil, to describe this transformation in the way in which we see ourselves, our world, and God. Second, Waugh speaks of "the delicious process of exploring [the Christian world] limitlessly." The creeds may offer us a snapshot of this vast landscape, but this is no substitute for inhabiting it and learning more about it firsthand. We can easily look admiringly at a photograph of the Alps, an African savannah, or a South Pacific coral island, but no photograph can hope to do justice to these evocative features of the natural world. We need to experience each of them and explore them for ourselves. The best theology arises from an extended intellectual habitation of the Christian faith.

The creeds are basically guidebooks to the landscape of faith. They map out the territory of the Christian faith and set an agenda for exploration and discovery. So what form of exploration are we talking about? The American novelist Henry Miller once said that "one's destination is never a place, but rather a new way of looking at things."[3] The Christian faith is like a lens that brings our world and our lives into focus, letting us look at things in a new way and see them more clearly as we journey through life. Even that journey itself is seen in a new way, allowing us to think of it as progress toward a goal rather than aimless meandering.

Christianity is thus, at least in part, about a transformed imaginative beholding of our world that allows us to see it as it really is rather than imprisoning us within a self-constructed world of delusion, no

21

matter how consoling this might be. The creeds provide us with a framework of meaning that allows and enables us to look at things we are familiar with, yet see them in a new light as we come to realize their true importance and value.

~~~~~~~~~

Now while this is an important point, it is also a very abstract point that clearly needs an illustration if it is to be properly grasped. So let me tell you the true story of a mysterious stone carving found in Canford School, in the southern English county of Dorset, which I had the pleasure of visiting recently. This school was founded in 1923 when Canford Manor, an old country house, was purchased and renovated for educational use. The house had previously been owned by a relative of Sir Henry Layard (1818–94), a prominent Victorian archaeologist who had spent much of his time excavating ancient sites in Mesopotamia and was credited with the discovery of the lost Assyrian city of Nineveh in 1845. Layard brought back a huge collection of Assyrian artifacts to England, most of which were installed at Canford Manor. After the First World War, many of these ended up in the British Museum in London or the Metropolitan Museum in New York.

In 1992, John M. Russell, a professor of art history at Columbia University who was researching a book about Layard, visited Canford School.[4] While exploring the school, he noticed a carved stone panel in the school's "tuck shop" (canteen). Like everyone else, he assumed that this was simply a modern cast of an ancient Assyrian carving. It had been painted with white emulsion paint. After a visit to the British Museum in London, he realized that it was actually a genuine three-thousand-year-old carved panel that Layard had brought back to England from the throne room of the Assyrian king Assurnasirpal II (883–859 BC). It was sold at auction in London in June 1994 for a record $11.8 million.

So what happened here? Did the stone panel itself change in order to acquire this value? No. Russell *recognized it for what it really was.* The key point is that the *stone was seen with new eyes.* Russell displayed what the philosopher Iris Murdoch (1919–99) called "attentiveness"—a careful, principled, committed attempt to perceive things as they really are rather than as they merely appear to be. The stone panel was seen in a new light, as Russell realized its true importance and value. The creeds offer us such an interpretative framework, a way of imagining ourselves and our worlds, that allows us to see both as they really are and thus live and act meaningfully.

~~~~~~~~~

Let me come back to the idea of the creeds as maps of faith. It's a helpful idea that ties in nicely with Ludwig Wittgenstein's idea of religious belief as "passionately committing oneself to a system of coordinates."[5] As every explorer will tell you, a good map is essential to help you get your bearings. Whether you are exploring a new land or trying to find your way home, the map will help you (if you know how to read it). A map shows you the big picture of the landscape, so you can work out where you are or what you're looking for. In the same way, the creeds give us a map of the Christian faith, so that we can explore it more fully.

Now I need to emphasize something that is very obvious but is too easily overlooked. Imagine somewhere special you've visited—perhaps a Caribbean island, an Umbrian landscape, or the mountains and forests of California. Can you remember what it was like to experience their natural beauty? Now imagine this same special place as it is depicted on a map. How does that two-dimensional representation compare with the three-dimensional reality? Not very well! A map cannot even begin to convey the vibrant colors, rich textures, and subtle fragrances of a glorious landscape. It cannot tell us what it is like to live there. Nor is a mere diagram on a piece of paper going to do justice to the beauty and majesty of the natural world. *But it's not meant to.*

Maps are just a reduced representation of a greater reality, a technical sketch of something vaster and more interesting. In a similar way, the creeds are a witness to faith and a convenient outline of the core elements of that faith, but they are not meant to—and they cannot—express the vibrancy, joy, and delight of the Christian faith. They are like fences enclosing the Christian pastureland or signposts telling us where to find water or food.

The words of the creeds never seem up to the serious job of capturing the rich Christian vision of reality in its totality. They seem to offer us a diminished and thin account of faith, and highlight the incapacity of human words to do justice to divine reality. Yet this will come as no surprise to those who reflect on the nature of human language. The philosopher Ludwig Wittgenstein famously pointed out that it was impossible even to convey the aroma of freshly ground coffee in words: "Describe the aroma of coffee. Why can't it be done? Do we lack the words? And for what are words lacking? But how do we get the idea that such a description must after all be possible? Have you ever felt the lack of such a description? Have you tried to describe the aroma of coffee and not succeeded?"[6]

The problem is not limited to communicating the smell of coffee. Imagine that you are standing on a mountain ridge in the Alps. Below you, spread out like a tapestry, is a beautiful landscape, stretching into the far distance. Woods, streams, fields, villages are all lit by the gentle radiance of a late afternoon sun. How would you describe this vista to someone back home? There is always going to be a significant imaginative gap between a word and the reality to which it points. You could tell your friend about a wood you saw in the distance from the mountaintop, but the little word "wood" will not capture your evocative memory of a green mass of trees, their dappled leaves shimmering in the sunlight, or your emotional reaction to this scene of beauty. At best, it can help you recover that memory, but it can never transmit it to others.

Yet this is not a fatal problem. It only becomes a real difficulty if we are unwise enough to assume an *identity* between the words of the creeds and the Christian faith—that is, if Christianity is understood simply as a checklist of verbal statements. Yet the creeds are intended to be seen as signposts, pointing to a greater reality that they cannot capture fully using the appointed means of their signification. The words are our attempts to express and communicate the deeper realities of faith. We must learn to see the creeds as verbal vessels signposting the treasure of the gospel. We need to look *at* them before moving on in order to look *through* them.

The map offered by the creeds distills the core themes of the Bible, disclosing a glorious, loving, and righteous God, who creates a world that goes wrong and then acts graciously and wondrously in order to renew and redirect before finally bringing it to its fulfillment. We are an integral part of this story, which discloses our true purpose, meaning, and value—who we are, what is wrong with us, what God proposes to do about this, and what we must do in response.

We must avoid thinking about Christian beliefs as if they were a set of individual, unrelated ideas. They are interconnected, like a spider's web, held together by the compelling and persuasive vision of reality that is made possible by the gospel. The Christian gospel is a totality that is greater than its individual components. Core themes of the Christian creeds—such as the doctrine of the Trinity, the incarnation, and the hope of heaven—should not be seen as self-contained, watertight compartments, each of which may be mastered without reference to anything else. We certainly need some manageable way of exploring the Christian faith. Yet this does not mean that we should think of Christianity as consisting of a series of individual, disconnected boxes, each of the contents of which may be inspected at any time without our needing to see what is contained in the others.

Let's change the analogy to help make this point clearer. Imagine that you are standing on a peak in the Swiss Alps or a hill in the Lake District. Below you, you see a breathtaking landscape. Wanting to capture its beauty and grandeur, you take snapshots of the individual elements of this landscape—rivers, villages, forests, and streams. Now imagine someone coming along with a much better camera than yours and taking a panoramic shot of the entire landscape. That person can capture the "big picture," of which your individual snapshots are parts. The panorama allows each of the snapshots to be fitted into the grander vision of the landscape, but on their own, your snapshots cannot disclose the panorama.

To make sense of the snapshots, we need to see how they fit into the panorama. Now there is nothing wrong with snapshots, which often provide welcome details of complex landscapes. Yet there is a risk that we will only see the snapshots and fail to see the bigger picture of which they are parts—but *only* parts. Too often we think of Christianity as a disconnected series of doctrinal statements and fail to join up the dots to grasp the bigger picture that they disclose. Yet, to understand individual Christian beliefs, we must first catch the greater vision of reality of which they are parts.

In thinking about any aspect of Christian belief—such as the doctrine of creation—we are really looking at one node of the web of faith or a single snapshot of the greater panorama of the gospel. To study any single Christian belief is actually to study the whole web of faith, the "grand narrative" of the gospel, as it intersects at this node or as it focuses on this theme. The image of a map helps us to realize how all the core beliefs of Christianity are woven together into an interconnected whole. The creeds are maps that help us to understand how ideas interconnect—just as maps show us how towns and cities are linked together by roads.

Let's remain with the image of the landscape for a moment longer, as there is another point that we need to consider. As we try to take in the vast, rich, and beautiful panorama that lies below us, most of us will find ourselves concentrating on one element of the vista that captures our attention, filtering out the rest. We may focus on a village in the distance, filtering out streams, pastures, and forests as we concentrate on this single facet of the panorama. This "selective attention" or "cognitive bias" is helpful in some ways. It allows us to focus on what we think really matters. Yet, all too often, it also means that we miss out on other aspects of that "big picture"—aspects that matter to other people and should probably matter to us as well.

That's why the community of faith matters. Imagine that you are joined by a group of friends as you look at the panorama. As you start talking to each other about what you see, it becomes clear that others have noticed things you missed. Where your attention focused on the village, others were fascinated by the iridescent rippling of a fast-flowing stream or the bucolic delight of some cattle finding shade under a tree from the hot afternoon sun. As you talk about what each of you saw, a communal view of the landscape emerges that is far more comprehensive and reliable than any individual account of it. Not only will a group see more than any single individual; a group may also correct an individual's account of the landscape of faith. What one person thought was a stream running through a wood might actually turn out to be a trail. We need a cumulative, comprehensive, and critical account of faith rather than being limited to one individual's often very subjective perception of things.

This reminds us that we should see the church as a community of learning, the wisdom and insights of that community transcending those of any one individual. Others who are journeying through the landscape of faith can help us as we travel with them, yet it is not only those around us who can help us. Those who have made the journey of faith before us can also help us as we undertake the same pilgrimage. They asked the same questions we ask, and their answers can encourage us as we wrestle today. As the great medieval theologian John of Salisbury remarked, "We are sitting on the shoulders of giants. We see more, and things that are more distant, than they did, not because our sight is superior or because we are taller than they were, but because they raise us up, and by their great stature add to ours."[7]

And that's what the creeds aim to do. The creeds are not personal statements of faith but, rather, are public statements of the faith of the Christian church that emerged within early communities of faith as they reflected on their rich heritage and sought to express this as succinctly as possible. The creeds sum up the Christian community's extended reflections on how best to make sense of the Bible and weave its multiple threads together to give the most satisfactory and authentic account of faith. None of those threads on its own would be adequate to disclose the greater picture of which it is a constituent part. As Cyril of Jerusalem pointed out in the fourth century, the creeds are essentially a "synthesis of faith" that set out the "teaching of the faith in its totality" by gathering together the core themes of the Bible and weaving them into a coherent whole.[8]

~~~~~~~~~

Some will still want to question the value of creeds in relation to Christian discipleship. For example, consider the calling of Peter and Andrew, the fishermen that Christ encountered on the shores of Lake Galilee (Mark 1:16–18). Christ speaks these simple words to them: "Come, follow me." They are not asked to accept—or recite—a creed; they are invited to follow him. The first disciples leave behind their nets—on which they depend completely to make a living—and follow this strange figure. They choose to entrust themselves totally to him, discerning that he is someone truly special.

So if the heart of faith is about entrusting ourselves to Jesus Christ, why make it more complicated by using creeds? Do we really need these uninviting verbalizations of faith, which often seem rather dull and wooden? These are perfectly reasonable questions. Yet we need to appreciate that, although Peter's and Andrew's journeys of faith may be said to have begun on the shores of Lake Galilee, they certainly did not end there. As we read the Gospels, we recognize that the disciples' faith deepens, both in terms of its *intensity* and its *substance*, as they gradually come to understand more about the identity and significance of Jesus of Nazareth and respond to him accordingly.

To begin with, Peter and Andrew trust Christ; as time passes, this personal trust is supplemented—*but is never displaced*—by beliefs about him. How did Christ fit into the story of Israel? What was so special about this person? What were the implications of following him? How did he fit into their own personal stories? Answering these questions leads to the emergence of a creed. Personal trust is enriched by a framework of beliefs. Jesus Christ stands at the center of a jigsaw puzzle. The rest of the pieces are put in place around him.

Whenever the disciples had to explain who Jesus Christ was or why he was so important, they found themselves having to use words to express their beliefs about him. The creeds are a network of carefully chosen words that the early church agreed on to try to capture what lay at the heart of the Christian faith, as a hedge encloses a pasture. They describe the Christian faith, as a sketch map describes a landscape.

~~~~~~

The creeds are statements of faith. Christian writers down the ages have distinguished two senses of this important word "faith." First, it can be understood as "a faith by which we believe"—that is to say, the act of trust and assent that says yes to God and reaches out to hold fast to God as the secure ground of life and thought. Second, it can be understood as a "faith we believe"—that is to say, a set of beliefs. In this sense of the word, "faith" refers to the content of what we believe rather than the act of believing and trusting. Although these two ways of understanding the word "faith" are inseparable, in that they are like two sides of the same coin, it is nevertheless helpful to distinguish between them. Creeds relate mainly to faith in the second sense of the word—but they nevertheless presuppose faith in the first sense.

We could thus make a distinction between "faith" (which is about relationships: "Whom do I *trust*?") and "belief" (which is about ideas: "What do I *think*?"). Using this framework, creeds are mainly about belief. Faith primarily describes a personal act of trust, a relationship with God, that is characterized by confidence, commitment, and love. To have faith in God is to place one's trust in God, believing that God is worthy of that trust. Beliefs represent an attempt to put the substance of that faith into words—in effect, explaining what it is about God that causes us to respond in an attitude of trust.

Now these creedal formulations may be secondary to the primary act of trust and commitment, but that does not mean they are unimportant or dispensable. The relationship between the believer and God, expressed in prayer and worship, calls out to be explored in words and ideas. Part of the life of faith is a desire to understand more about who and what we trust. The medieval theologian Anselm of Canterbury (c. 1033–1109) famously expressed this point in his slogan *fides quarens intellectum*, "faith seeking understanding."

~~~~~~~~

Let me now pick up on a phrase I used earlier, which needs to be explored in more detail. I suggested that we need to learn to see *through* the creeds. What did I mean by that? I have taught theology for many years at Oxford University and have learned that there are three main questions we should ask about any doctrine of the Christian faith—such as the Trinity. First, we ask why this doctrine is to be believed—in other words, What are the reasons for thinking that this is justified and trustworthy? Second, we move on to ask how this doctrine might be taught or preached. What analogies might we use to help make sense of it? Third, we ask a deeper question. If this doctrine is indeed right, what difference does it make to the way we understand ourselves and our world? How does it shape the way in which we live?

It is this third question that I want to consider in more detail now. Christian discipleship is about reflective inhabitation of our faith. Christianity gives us a lens through which we can see ourselves and our world for what they really are. One of the finest statements of this principle is found in the poetry of George Herbert (1593–1633), especially in these lines:

> A man that looks on glass,
>   On it may stay his eye;
> Or if he pleaseth, through it pass,
>   And then the heav'n espy.[9]

Herbert was writing in the early seventeenth century, when two inventions that made use of lenses—often referred to as "glasses" at that time—were transforming human appreciation of the natural world. He draws a clear distinction between the different modes of viewing these allow: *looking at* and *looking through*. You can look at a microscope or a telescope. Alternatively, you can look through them and find yourself in a new world.

In Herbert's day, the microscope allowed a new wealth of detail to be seen in the petals of flowers and the wings of butterflies, while the telescope revealed the moons of the planet Jupiter and the mass of stars that make up the Milky Way. Both instruments allowed people to view things that had always been there but previously had not been visible because they lay beyond the frontiers of human vision. We could not see them because our eyes were not good enough. An expansion of vision was needed to open up these new worlds.

Herbert's comments, however, are primarily about theology and concern the purpose and place of Christian beliefs. He helps us to understand that we can approach beliefs in two ways. First, we can look *at* them—an approach found in many traditional textbooks of theology, which set out each individual Christian doctrine and allow its distinct themes to be appreciated. Second, we can look *through* them, as if they were a telescope enabling us to "the heav'n espy," and enjoy an enriched view of reality, resulting from a heightened ability to discern what is really there.

Embracing Christianity's "bigger picture" helps us to realize that each of us, being created in God's image, matters profoundly; and that status and wealth mean nothing compared to the riches of knowing God. As Thomas à Kempis (c. 1380–1471) pointed out in his spiritual classic *The Imitation of Christ*, when seen in a right perspective, "the glory of the world fades away."[10] We see things from a new perspective and come to realize that this is not just a different way of looking at our world—it is a faithful and critical account of the way the world really is. Christian discipleship involves reflecting on the new world that is opened up as we look *through* the creeds *at* the world and ourselves, and come to see them in a new way.

Yet we need to appreciate that some people choose to keep seeing the world using a distorting mirror or turn a blind eye toward the darker side of human nature. The philosopher Iris Murdoch often pointed out that human beings find reality somewhat uncomfortable and prefer to invent ways of looking at their world and themselves that are less disturbing to them. Looking at things through a Christian lens, however, brings our true situation into focus, enabling us to realize that we cannot go on as we are. To use a medical analogy, the Christian framework of meaning acts as a diagnostic tool, showing us that something is wrong with us and telling us the treatment required if we are to be cured. We are liberated from the delusion that all is well and shown what needs to be done if things are to be put right.

Let me conclude by asking a practical question. How can we use the creeds to develop our own personal faith, in terms of both its breadth and depth? One important way is to see the creeds as mapping the landscape of faith, and inviting us to explore it, in the full knowledge that there are parts of the landscape that remain unfamiliar to us. I see the creeds as inviting me to explore what I have not yet encountered and affirm what I have not yet understood. The creeds are *aspirational*, in that they set out a vision that they invite us to share, even though many of us are still exploring individual aspects of that vision.

At its best, Christian theology can do three things, all of which are the natural and proper outcomes of reflecting on the creeds. Let me note these briefly.

1. It allows the Christian community to preserve its distinct identity, by reaffirming the core beliefs that stand at its heart.
2. It enables the church to look outward, by providing a secure intellectual basis for engaging alternative ways of seeing our world. Theology offers Christians an intellectual foundation for apologetics—a positive interaction with our wider culture, in which life's "ultimate questions" can be probed and answered.
3. It offers individual believers a resource for the further exploration of their faith, allowing us to become more deeply embedded within the Christian vision of reality. Christian theology thus both stimulates and nourishes Christian discipleship.

The Spanish writer Teresa of Ávila's landmark work *The Interior Castle of the Soul* (1577) suggests that we think of faith as the exploration of a castle. Having been granted access, we yearn (and are meant to yearn) to explore the castle's inner courtyards, one by one. Teresa insists that we must be careful never to limit the Christian vision of reality to that which we have personally experienced, understood, or grasped. Others, past and present, urge us to go further and deeper, opening up other rooms in the "castle of the soul" as we explore the "boundless riches of Christ" (Eph. 3:8). We are to be caught up in the reflective inhabitation of something that is greater and more wonderful than we initially realize.

Reciting the creeds is thus about both affirming what we have already discovered and come to trust, and setting an agenda for the enlargement of our appreciation of God and Christ. It reminds us of both what we know and what we need to discover. The creeds might not offer us a definitive account of the "boundless riches of Christ," but they provide a framework for discovering and appreciating these, as part of the ongoing process of Christian discipleship. May that journey of exploration continue!

3

Habits of the Christian Mind

The Community of Faith and Personal Growth

M y topic in this chapter is the role of the community of
faith—the church—in the process of Christian discipleship.
For C. S. Lewis, reflecting on his own experience of spiritual growth and theological reflection, it seemed clear that "the one
really adequate instrument for learning about God is the Christian
community."[1] So how are we to understand the role of the church in
developing habits of thought that are rooted in the fundamentals of
the Christian faith? In this chapter, I want to highlight one aspect of
the identity of the church, firmly rooted in its history, that I believe
to be important for both Christian discipleship and the witness of
the church to the world—namely, understanding the church as a
visionary community, enabling us to see the world and ourselves
in a new and compelling light, and to sustain this sense of wonder
through worship and adoration.

Based on a talk given to Christian graduate students at Oxford University in June
2016.

The Christian Vision: On Seeing Things as They Really Are

The New Testament affirms that the human situation is transformed by the Christian gospel. This renewal and regeneration is not restricted to moral and relational matters but also extends to the way that we think about ourselves and our world, summed up in Paul's great injunction to his readers to be actively "transformed by the renewing of your minds" rather than being passively "conformed to this world" (Rom. 12:2). The New Testament uses a wide range of images to describe this change, many of which suggest a change to the way in which we see the world. Our eyes are healed so that we might see properly; a veil is removed so that obstacles to our beholding of God's world might be removed. For the New Testament, such a process of transformation is invariably seen as a gracious act of God rather than something that we can do by ourselves.

This radical reorientation of the human understanding and manner of beholding the world is often described by the New Testament and early Christian writers as *metanoia*—a Greek word traditionally translated as "repentance," yet its full meaning is probably better expressed as a "transformation of the mind."[2] For those who have experienced a dramatic moment of conversion, this takes the form of disruption of a settled secular habit of thought, leading to the development of a habit of the mind that is rooted in and informed by the Christian faith. For others, it is about continued growth in their faith, in which our minds and imaginations become saturated and infused with the realities of the Christian faith.

This is not an instantaneous event but, rather, is a gradual process of transformation that requires nourishment and development through discipline and practice. The New Testament uses a series of analogies to speak of such intellectual and spiritual disciplines, such as an athlete in training for a race and a soldier negotiating the boundaries between his civilian and military commitments (1 Cor.

9:24–26; 2 Tim. 2:3–4). We may embrace Christ in conversion, yet this act of commitment is followed by an extended exploration of the landscape of faith, which we have now made our home.[3]

Paul's concept of the "mind of Christ" is open to a number of interpretations,[4] but is perhaps most naturally understood as a settled way of thinking, capable of expansion and consolidation, which allows our experience of the world to be structured and consolidated within the framework of the Christian faith. Through faith, Christians develop habits of engagement with our world that allow it to be seen, understood, and evaluated in new ways. While this process of transformation and growth takes place within the individual believer, it is encouraged and informed by the community of faith as a whole.

This important point was emphasized by Augustine of Hippo, who argued that the Christian church and its ministers had a critically important role to play in encouraging and sustaining the intellectual, moral, and spiritual transformation of believers: "Our whole business in this life is to heal the eye of the heart [*sanare oculum cordis*] in order that God may be seen. It is for this reason that the holy mysteries are celebrated and the word of God is preached, and it is towards this goal that the moral exhortations of the church are directed."[5]

Augustine's arresting phrase "heal the eye of the heart"—which draws on the imagery of Ephesians 1:18—suggests that gaining these new habits of thought can be compared to a blind person being enabled to see and appreciate the world for the first time. The true beauty of the world is hidden from us until we are enabled to see it properly. Yet while God is the ultimate enabler of the process of healing and renewal that allows us to see things as they really are, other agencies are involved in the mediation of this transformation—above all, the Christian church.

Augustine sees the Christian community as playing a critical role in this process by reinforcing this way of seeing things by its proclamation and sacramental ministries, which both narrate and enact this vision of reality, correlating it with human experience. Rowan Williams expresses much the same idea when he speaks of discipleship as a process of formation and discernment by which "the particularities of experience are brought slowly into interconnection with the communally-confessed truth of God's nature and activity."[6]

A similar point is made by the American theologian Stanley Hauerwas, who stressed the importance of developing and maintaining a distinctively Christian approach to ethics. Once more, we find an emphasis on the distinctiveness of the Christian way of seeing (and hence evaluating) the world. We need a framework or lens through which we may "see" the world of human behavior.[7] This is provided by sustained, detailed, extended reflection on the Christian narrative, which is articulated and enacted in the life and witness of the church: "The primary task of Christian ethics involves an attempt to help us see. For we can only act within the world we can see, and we can only see the world rightly by being trained to see. We do not come to see just by looking, but by disciplined skills developed through initiation into a narrative."[8]

The Christian church thus embodies a way of seeing the world that is proclaimed and sustained by its controlling words, images, and actions. There is an obvious correlation here with Alasdair MacIntyre's insights into how communities maintain their identity through "habits" of thought and action, which are mediated through traditions.[9] We are thus called on to see the world in its true light, by adopting a Christian "mental map" that enables the world to be illuminated and brought into focus, so it may be seen as it really is. Hauerwas thus insists that "the church serves the world by giving the world the means to see itself truthfully."[10]

The church can thus act as a channel of spiritual insight or as a lens of theological vision. As Austin Farrer once remarked, we "see through the Church of Christ as a man sees through the telescope to the stars."[11] To speak of the church as a community of theological "vision," however, transcends the task of making sense of the present, in that the church also looks ahead to a better, transformed future, shaped by the Christian hope. The church has a role to play as a sign, instrument, and foretaste of the kingdom of God,[12] pointing toward the renewal of humanity's hopes and the transformation of its situation through grace. The church possesses the capacity to disclose this better future and to model and embody this in its witness to the world. The church both anticipates the coming of the New Jerusalem in its proclamation and worship, and seeks to embody and exhibit its values in the present.

The Christian Vision and the Transformation of Reality

My core argument in this chapter is that the Christian faith offers a way of seeing reality that brings about a transformation and reevaluation of our understanding of the world and our place within it. It strips away our delusions about reality, illuminating it and bringing it into sharp focus so that we may see it as it really is. The Christian church is a community that has been molded by this vision and that in turn bears witness to its capacity to illuminate and transform.

The language of "seeing" reality calls into question the adequacy of simply "thinking about" our world. Christian discipleship is imaginative, not simply rational, demanding expansion of the capacity of all our faculties—reason, imagination, and emotions—to accommodate the rich and overwhelming vision of God set out in the New Testament and enacted in the worship and proclamation of the church. This imaginatively compelling and intellectually enriching vision of reality is mediated by the community of faith. Individual believers are thus reflective inhabitants of this tradition, simultaneously being nourished by its received wisdom and invited to deepen their appreciation of its vision of the gospel through attentive reflection (1 Thess. 5:21).

We might think of the church as an "interpretive community," to use a term favored by the literary critic Stanley Fish,[13] that crystallizes around and proclaims a particular "point of view or way of organizing experience."[14] The Christian church can thus be seen as an interpretive community that crystallizes around what Rowan Williams styles "the one focal interpretive story of Jesus"[15]—a particular interpretation of the texts of Scripture, history, and nature, understood in terms of the life, death, and resurrection of Jesus Christ, or a trinitarian "economy of salvation" of creation, redemption, and consummation.

The community of faith thus sees the world in a manner that differs strikingly from what Charles Taylor termed the prevailing "social imaginaries," a term he uses to designate the ways in which people imagine their social existence.[16] The church should therefore proclaim, exhibit, and embody its own "social imaginary," which is deeply rooted in the gospel. Christians and others engage with the same empirical realities—what we might loosely call "the world"— but they nevertheless see (and hence understand and evaluate) them in very different ways.

"Nature" is thus seen in different ways by communities or individuals, in that they observe the natural world through different theoretical lenses, which shape what they "see."[17] The term "nature" thus denotes a variety of ways in which human observers choose to see, interpret, and inhabit the empirical world. The question concerns the best or most appropriate lens or interpretative framework through which we are to behold the natural world. The issue will be familiar from the philosophy of science. The great nineteenth-century philosopher of science William Whewell (1794–1866) pointed out that there is "a mask of theory over the whole face of nature."[18] More recently, the philosopher of science N. R. Hanson has argued persuasively that the process of observation is "theory-laden."[19]

Christianity offers us a theoria, a "sort of intellectual seeing"[20]— a way of beholding our world that interprets and values the natural world as God's creation, with an imparted capacity to disclose the

God who created it. We might think here of the moral philosopher R. M. Hare, who wrote of the importance of what he termed a "blik"—a way of envisaging reality meaningfully, which gave him confidence to live and think morally rather than being forced to rely on the severely limited deliverances of possible sense experience.[21]

In part, we evaluate a theory by trying to work out its capacity to enable us to see something more clearly, more comprehensively, more plausibly, and more fruitfully. A good theory enriches our vision of reality rather than limiting itself to "saving the phenomena." This point was appreciated by Iris Murdoch, who spoke of the need to see beyond the realm of the empirical to discern deeper truths about the world beyond its horizon. Such an act of informed imagination, she argues, is able to go beyond "what could be said to be strictly factual"; it is thus to be contrasted with "strict" or "scientific" thinking, which focuses on a surface reading of things.[22] This deeper engagement with reality allows us legitimately to construct meaning and value rather than contenting ourselves with the mere identification of natural mechanisms and processes.

Three Elements of the Discipleship of the Mind

Christianity offers us a mental map of reality, which it affirms to be truthful and trustworthy. Part of the discipleship of faith is the exploration and appreciation of the "coherence of Christian doctrine,"[23] which is best thought of as an interconnected web of ideas. This process of exploration can be thought of as having three main elements.[24]

In the first place, we must consider the reasons for believing that a certain doctrine is true. What are the warrants for accepting its trustworthiness? A major responsibility of Christian theology is to explore the web of ideas that enfold the Christian experience of the living God, and demonstrate their interconnectedness and dependence, as well as their plausibility and reliability. The church must

41

therefore respond to challenges to belief from outside the church (for example, the New Atheist critique of the rationality of the Trinity) and reassure Christians of the intrinsic coherence of their faith. The community of faith thus provides a "plausibility structure" for faith,[25] gathering together a group of people who share and affirm the Christian vision, which is reinforced and consolidated by word and sacrament, and exhibited in attitudes and actions.

In the second place, we must consider how best we can express and communicate these ideas. The history of Christian theology is rich in analogies and images designed to help believers grasp some of the truths of faith. For example, Gregory of Nyssa developed a series of analogies to enable his audiences to cope with the challenges of the doctrine of the Trinity, including the oft-cited analogy of a spring, fount, and stream of water.

There is also a third task, which is often overlooked. If a given doctrine is true, *what are its implications?* What difference does the Christian faith make to the way in which we understand our world and act within it? What new or distinctive way of seeing things does it enable and how does this affect our behavior? If we see the world as God's creation, how does that alter our behavior toward it? It is not difficult to see how a basic environmental ethic emerges from this process of reflection. Yet perhaps more importantly, the process of reflection both expresses and affirms the interconnection of what Christians believe and how Christians live.

The Church and the World: Distinct but Not Disconnected

While the Christian church engages the same empirical realities as everyone else, it interprets, experiences, and evaluates them in ways that diverge significantly from the shallow rationalism that has become the default setting for contemporary cultural norms.[26] Yet this distinct way of interpreting and inhabiting the world is maintained without entailing, or even encouraging, a disconnection on the part of the Christian community from shared human experiences and concerns. This point is of vital importance in understanding how the church can maintain its distinct identity without becoming separated and isolated from the broader world of human culture and experience. We shall explore this point further in what follows.

While the church is called to be distinct from the world, it is also called to serve that world in many ways, including proclaiming the good news of Jesus Christ. As Rowan Williams notes, "The Church . . . is essentially missionary in its nature, seeking to transform the human world by communicating to it in word and act a truthfulness that exposes the deepest human fears and evasions and makes possible the kind of human existence that can pass beyond these fears to a new liberty."[27]

Yet it is alarmingly easy to move from being *distinct* from the world to being *disconnected* from the world, having no shared language or values, no point of contact, with culture at large. A church that emphasizes its distinctiveness from the world while failing to connect with it simply becomes a ghetto, isolated from the mainstream of culture and unable to speak meaningfully to it, let alone influence or redirect its course.

This is a familiar point, often expressed in the somewhat dull and predictable theological platitude that the church is *in* the world but not *of* the world. The church finds itself in a creative tension between maintaining its distinctiveness on the one hand and its capacity to engage with its cultural context on the other. So how can the church be both culturally relevant (contextualized) and at the same time countercultural (gospel centered)? How can it be distinct from its context, yet remain connected to or embedded within it? How can the church remain firmly in the public square rather than in some isolated ghetto with its own private language and habits of thought that many of our contemporaries, whether with affection or derision, see as quaint relics of a discarded past?

Both individual Christians and the church journey through the same natural landscape as everyone else. Yet while the church shares in this common experience of humanity, it brings to bear on it an interpretative framework that allows this journey to be understood and evaluated in a new way. It offers a vision that we believe and trust to be imaginatively compelling, that has the capacity to attract others to this pilgrim community of faith as it passes through this world.

The church thus invites others to "try seeing things this way,"[28] trusting that the outcome of this process of reflection will be the realization of the viability and potency of this vision of reality. The imagination is thus a gateway to faith, allowing people outside the church to catch a glimpse of the "vision glorious" of human existence that faith offers. For some, it is the truth of faith that attracts; for others, however, the attraction of faith is found to lie in its outcomes.

The Place of Worship in Discipleship

Earlier, I raised the question of the tension between deepening our understanding of our faith and becoming entrapped in a shallow and superficial rationalism. It is a real risk. Human beings are very good at limiting reality to what they can comprehend and constructing impoverished and truncated worlds that turn out to be little more than prisons of the mind. Instead of limiting reality to what we can comprehend, we ought to be expanding our vision of reality by contemplating the vastness of the universe and the glory of God—two trajectories of thought that coalesce in the psalmist's celebrated declaration that "the heavens are telling the glory of God" (Ps. 19:1).

In the natural sciences, we often have to face up to the inadequacy of the human mind to take in the vastness and complexity of our universe. Acknowledging this, Richard Dawkins emphasizes the need to recognize the validity of the category of "mystery" in science:

"Modern physics teaches us that there is more to truth than meets the eye; or than meets the all too limited human mind, evolved as it was to cope with medium-sized objects, moving at medium speeds through medium distances in Africa."[29] To limit reality to what the "all too limited human mind" can cope with is to diminish our world. We must be challenged, on the contrary, to expand our intellectual vision, even if this causes us mental discomfort.

There is, of course, an obvious parallel in the world of theology: the importance of worship as an expression of the glory and majesty of God and our inability to comprehend or express this fully. Worship both expresses and helps to shape a faithful Christian imagination, which shakes off the restrictions of inadequate and limited conceptions of God and invites us to apprehend and embrace the greater reality disclosed and expressed through the church's adoration. The Christian practice of worship emerges from its theological vision of reality and expresses that vision in an imaginatively and emotionally powerful—yet appropriate—way. The worship of the church invites us to cultivate a receptivity to mystery,[30] encouraging us to expand our minds to appreciate a glorious and majestic reality that is greater than our capacity to comprehend it fully.

The word "glory" is viewed with suspicion by some today, but we need to keep on using it and keep on appreciating it. The term "glory" expresses the "weightiness," the infinite beauty and greatness, of God—something that is simply too great for us to take in. Glory is about the intellectual and imaginative capacity of God to overwhelm us, reminding us that our attempts to capture God's nature in human words can only end in frustration.

It is no accident that so many theologians have seen an analogy between Jacob's wrestling with a mysterious figure at Peniel (Gen. 32:24–32) and the human struggle to do justice to God. Just as Jacob withdrew from this struggle, wounded and defeated, so theologians must also recognize the limits placed on their discipline. Theology is perhaps one of the few disciplines that transforms intellectual defeat into a virtue, precisely because it discloses the limits placed on human reason and the folly of relying too much on it.

That's why good theology leads to worship, in that it confronts us with a vision of God so compelling and overwhelming that we cannot help but adore it on the one hand and fail to put it into words on the other. Theology informs our minds without limiting reality to what our minds can enfold, thus alerting us to a greater horizon of divine activity and presence that is best expressed in worship and adoration rather than in theological speculation. To borrow a phrase from John Henry Newman, it is through the devotional, spiritual, prayerful practice of Christianity that we come to have a "real apprehension" (rather than a purely "notional apprehension") of what theology is all about.[31]

Conclusion

In this chapter, I have emphasized one aspect of the church's distinctive role—to function as a community of discernment, enabling the growth in faith that is integral to Christian discipleship. I appreciate that some of the ideas and writers I have explored here are intellectually demanding and are often expressed in somewhat opaque ways; nevertheless, I am offering them to you precisely because I have found them helpful in my own reflections and would like to offer them to you in case they may be helpful to you as well. It is my hope that the approaches I have outlined in this chapter may serve both to deepen the quality of the Christian life of the mind within the church on the one hand and to enable the church to discourse persuasively with its fellow travelers about the meaning and goals of life on the other.

4

Books and the Discipleship
of the Mind

Alonso of Arragon was wont to say in commendation of age,
that age appears best in four things: old wood best to burn, old
wine to drink, old friends to trust and old authors to read.

Francis Bacon, *Aphorisms and Apothegms*[1]

These words of the Renaissance philosopher Francis Bacon
came to mind as I began to think about what I might say, not
just in honoring my friend Bill Reimer, the longtime manager
of the famous bookshop at Regent College, Vancouver, but also
reflecting on the wider significance of books in relation to Christian
discipleship. One of the things that I most looked forward to during
my visits to Regent College was spending time with Bill, musing on

A paper written in 2017 for the students and faculty at Regent College, Vancouver,
in celebration of Bill Reimer, the longtime manager of its famous bookshop. This
essay was originally published in *Crux*, a journal of Christian thought and opinion
published by the Faculty and Alumni of Regent College, Vancouver, BC, Canada,
and is reproduced with permission.

the complex and shifting worlds of publishing and bookselling. As an author, I valued his wisdom and insights. Bill has managed to sustain a bookshop in the midst of cultural and economic turbulence and change, offering both the college and the Canadian Christian community a significant theological and spiritual resource. In honoring him and reflecting on our shared passion for books, I offer the following thoughts on why books still matter and what we can learn from them.

~~~~~~~~

Books open our minds and our imaginations, allowing us to see God and our world as others see them and reflect on what we find. The French novelist Marcel Proust spoke of the "only true voyage of discovery" being "not to travel to new landscapes, but to possess other eyes, to behold the universe through the eyes of another, of a hundred others."[2] Whatever else they may be, gifted authors are fundamentally people who have seen something others have missed and enable us to grasp and appreciate this new way of seeing things in and through their writings. The best writers are not self-promoting narcissists who demand that we look at *them*, but those who invite us to look through them at *what they have seen*, so that we too might share in their experience. They are windows to something that is greater. Those who have seen this before us thus stand to one side so that we might see where they are pointing rather than be distracted by them.

It's a wonderful thought: the possibility of transcending our own limitations by looking at the world as others see it, allowing their vision of things to enrich or challenge our own. As C. S. Lewis pointed out, this kind of literary engagement "heals the wound, without undermining the privilege, of individuality." In reading great literature, Lewis found that he was able to transcend his limits, while still remaining himself: "Like the night sky in the Greek poem, I see with a myriad eyes, but it is still I who see."[3] Lewis himself saw authors not as spectacles to be admired, but as a "set of spectacles" through which we can look at the world and see it in sharper focus and increased depth of field.

For so many, as for Lewis, an engagement with literature is a gateway to the enrichment of our vision, allowing us to see things that we had hitherto missed; perhaps it might challenge our ideas and force us to review them, considering alternatives that had hitherto been seen as unthinkable. That was certainly Lewis's own experience at Oxford in the early 1920s, as he began to immerse himself in the study of English literature. As he reflected on the varying quality of literary representations of reality, Lewis came to realize that those of modernist writers such as George Bernard Shaw and H. G. Wells "seemed a little thin," lacking depth or any capacity to comprehend the complexity of real life. The shallow rationalist mind-set that they embodied seemed to be unable to cope with the "roughness and density of life." Yet, to his evident surprise, the still-atheist Lewis came to realize that what he then called "the Christian mythology"—as expressed, for example, in the writings of George Herbert—seemed to excel as a medium for "conveying the very quality of life as we actually live it."[4] Lewis's love of literature was thus integral to his later discovery of the rational and imaginative appeal of Christianity. As he later said, "A young man who wishes to remain a sound Atheist cannot be too careful of his reading. There are traps everywhere."[5]

I too experienced this capacity of books to break spells and open up new ways of visualizing and inhabiting our world. Like many young people in the late 1960s, I regarded the idea of God as outdated nonsense. This was a time of intellectual and cultural change, in which the traditional "certainties" of the past became increasingly precarious and unsettled. By the age of sixteen, I was convinced that the natural sciences alone could satisfy our intellectual longings and answer our deepest questions. If science could not answer a question, it was not a real question in the first place. I took it as a self-evident truth that science entailed atheism. Where some railed against the metaphysical austerity of a godless world, I took my cues from Nietzsche, seeing atheism as a bold assertion of meaninglessness, a distinguishing mark of intellectual bravery and integrity.

My future, it seemed to me then, lay in the study of science, which I confidently expected to lead to an interesting career on the one hand, and the intellectual confirmation and consolidation of my atheism on the other. To my delight, I learned that I had won a scholarship to Oxford University to study chemistry, with effect from October 1971. In the meantime, I decided that I would use my remaining time at school to extend my reading in aspects of science.

After a month or so of intensive reading in the school's science library, I came across a collection of dust-shrouded books in a battered bookcase labeled "The History and Philosophy of Science." I was suspicious back then of both history and philosophy, tending to see them as uninformed criticism of the certainties and simplicities of the natural sciences by those who felt threatened by them. Philosophy, in my view, was just pointless speculation about issues that any proper scientist could solve easily through a few well-designed experiments. What was the point? In the end, however, I decided to work my way through these volumes. If I was right, what had I to lose by doing so, apart from some time?

By the time I had finished reading those books, I realized that I needed to do some very serious rethinking. Far from being half-witted obscurantism that placed unnecessary obstacles in the place of relentless scientific advance, the history and philosophy of science asked all the right questions about the reliability and limits of scientific knowledge—questions that I had not faced thus far. I was forced to confront the awkward realities of the underdetermination of theory by data, the phenomenon of radical theory change in the history of science, the difficulties in devising a "crucial experiment," and the enormously complex issues associated with devising what was the "best explanation" of a given set of observations. I was overwhelmed by an intellectual tidal wave, battering my settled way of thinking, muddying what I had taken to be the clear, still, and above all, *simple* waters of scientific truth.

Things thus turned out to be rather more complicated than I realized. I had enjoyed the beauty and innocence of a childlike attitude to the sciences and secretly wished to remain in that secure place, but those books opened my eyes. I knew there was—and could be—no going back to the simplistic take on the natural sciences that I had once taken for granted. I could not escape the new world I now began to inhabit. I had lost my epistemic innocence and had to find my way through the irrefractable and irreducible landscape of a grown-up world. I had once breezily dismissed Bertrand Russell's suggestion that philosophy tries to teach us "how to live without certainty, and yet without being paralysed by hesitation."[6] I could now see his point, which cut the ground from under my simplistic certainties, demanding a more nuanced and cautious engagement with reality.

I found that I could no longer hold on to what I now realize was a somewhat naive scientific positivism. It became clear to me that a whole series of questions that I had dismissed as meaningless or pointless had to be examined again—including the God question. I did not turn from atheism to Christianity as a result of reading those books. Rather, they forced me to realize that atheism was a faith, a belief that could not be proved to be true. Science was more intellectually malleable than I had realized. It did not entail atheism or, indeed, any religious or antireligious ideology. It was just science and had to be respected as such.

So if atheism was actually a faith, should I not reconsider other faiths that I had earlier dismissed *precisely because they were faiths*? I first began to grasp the intellectual depth and resilience of the Christian faith during my first term at Oxford University, but my earlier reading of the books mentioned above had prepared the way for this breakthrough. It broke the spell of scientific atheism and opened my eyes to deeper and richer ways of thinking about science.

The traps Lewis had warned of were the traps into which I fell—and from which I emerged a wiser person.

~~~~~~~~~~

As I began to grow in my faith, I found myself drawn toward the study of Christian theology. After all, we are told that the process of Christian discipleship engages and makes demands of all our faculties: "You shall love the Lord your God with all your heart, and with all your soul, and with all your mind, and with all your strength" (Mark 12:30). We are called to love God with all of our minds: to *think* about our faith. When rightly understood—and it is so easily misunderstood—theology is about an imaginative enlargement of our vision of God and the corresponding expansion of our mental capacity to grasp and appreciate the rich and rewarding "big picture" of reality that lies at the heart of the Christian faith.

Christian theology is the natural and necessary outcome of our personal encounter and sustained engagement with the person of Jesus Christ. We are drawn to the Gospel accounts of Christ, finding that he appeals to something deep within us. Yet we need to try to put into words precisely what it is that we have found and ask how what others have found could further enrich our own experience and understanding of the Christian faith. We Christians are the wandering people of God, sojourners and wayfarers in our strange world, whose shared vision of the meaning of life and the hope of glory keeps us going as we travel through a landscape that is so often shrouded in mist and darkness. And those who have traveled this road before us are able to pass down to us their wisdom and insights.

While I have gained much from conversations about faith from my fellow travelers through the landscape of the Christian faith, I have found that my personal faith is now enriched and deepened mainly by reading books. Although many other books have helped me, I have come to see that Bacon was right: there is something special about having "old authors to read"—not least because the best of the more recent books so often represent reworkings and reappropriations of those older ideas and approaches.

So why do I take such pleasure in reading the works of long-dead authors, such as Irenaeus of Lyons, Augustine of Hippo, and Athanasius of Alexandria? Books become classics for a reason—namely, that people continue to find in them something of value and excellence, to which they return again and again. Classic writers help us to break free from our naive assumption that the most recent is the best; that the wisdom of the past is somehow discredited or eclipsed by more recent writing. Newer books are in the process of being assessed: some will stand the test of time, others will not. The greatest challenge a book faces is perhaps not how it is judged today, but how it will be judged a generation from now. Will it be valued? Will it be remembered at all?

The Christian classics—such as Athanasius's *On the Incarnation* or Augustine's *Confessions*—possess the ability to tether us to our collective past, offering us resources that inform us about our faith while also revealing the blind spots of our own chronological parochialism. They anchor us to a continuous tradition of reflection, allowing us to see the great questions and problems of our own time and culture through the eyes of others. As Lewis observed in his own introduction to Athanasius's *On the Incarnation*, we need to "keep the clean sea breeze of the centuries blowing through our minds, and this can be done only by reading old books."[7] One of the chief values of old literature lies in its ability to expose the assumptions that we so often take for granted as self-evidently correct, but are actually culturally situated and will one day seem strange to future generations.

Let me note one of those fashionable assumptions that would have seemed strange in the past and, I suspect (and hope), will seem strange in the future as well: that we can invent our own intellectual and moral worlds. It seems to me that some now inhabit a "post-truth" world, in which people simply make up their most cherished beliefs and see this as entirely reasonable and straightforward. We create a world that fits in with our preconceived ideas or our deepest longings and take offense when our imagined certainties are challenged. Why worry about someone else's so-called reality when we can create our own and subjugate our perceptions to our longings? T. S. Eliot was prophetic in his suggestion that we "cannot bear very much reality."[8] Yet Eliot seemed to be objecting to an evasion of reality, whereas many now deny the existence of *any* reality, save that which they have personally constructed.

One of the more disturbing characteristics of this post-truth age is that people limit themselves to their own narrow communities, regarding connection or communication with other communities as signs of intellectual contamination or cultural degradation. We all too often live in self-reinforcing and self-referential intellectual and cultural bubbles, members of "in-groups" who demonize inferior "out-groups," thus dividing the world into heroes and villains and unproblematically locating ourselves among the former. We read only "approved" newspapers and "safe" web postings from "trusted" authors, anxious to avoid any hint that we might recognize good or truth in others, which would invariably lead to a humiliating ejection from our favored "in-group."

That's why we need to read books. They put us in touch with a wider world. They force us to confront and evaluate alternative views of the world and ways of inhabiting it. They invite us to listen to forgotten, marginalized, or suppressed viewpoints. We can indeed criticize views we find uncomfortable or wrong; we cannot, however, haughtily dismiss them with the scorn that was such a trademark of the New Atheism of Richard Dawkins or Christopher Hitchens—an intellectual embarrassment that is now happily receding into the distance. Hitchens believed that a contemptuous dismissal of religion signaled intellectual virtue on his part, when it was actually a sign of prejudice-fueled superficiality, woodenly and predictably compliant with the norms of his cultural "in-group."

Lewis was right in his suggestion that those who call themselves "freethinkers" are so often the willing prisoners of a "glib and shallow rationalism."[9] Books invite us to imagine new worlds and new ways of thinking. The New Atheism seems to think it can only survive by censoring our reading habits and suppressing our imaginations. Both Lewis and I came to faith through reading books, realizing that they raised questions about the reliability and coherence of our earlier atheism. So why, I often wonder, are so many Christians reluctant to use literature as an apologetic gateway? Why do so many of us share the seventeenth-century Puritan writer Richard Baxter's superficial judgment that, since literature is fictional, it engenders and encourages falsities? Surely there is more that needs to be done here.

<hr />

A powerful objection might be raised here, rightly demanding our consideration. "What you say is all very well, but why books? Why not just use the online text of those books? Surely they convey exactly the same information but in a much more convenient form?" It is an entirely fair objection. Why do we need the bulky physical objects that we call "books" when their content is easily available in a more modern and compact format? So let me explain why I think there continues to be something about books that gives them a distinct place in our lives.

First, when I buy a book, it becomes mine. When I was younger (and poorer), I used to write my name inside the cover of every book I bought, alongside the date and place of its purchase. So, reaching into my hopelessly disorganized accumulation of books (which is so chaotic I could not really describe it as a "library"), I can see that I bought Karl Barth's *Epistle to the Romans* in Blackwell's bookshop, Oxford, on September 29, 1973, and Thomas F. Torrance's *Theological Science* in Heffer's bookshop, Cambridge, on June 2, 1979. Those books became part of my own story as I discovered and absorbed new ideas and tried to work out how they fitted into my own journey of faith. They are milestones along my own road of reflection, marking moments when I invited these writers to become my conversation partners in my evolving exploration of the Christian faith.

As I browse through my bookshelves, I find myself reconstructing my own intellectual journey and its moments of illumination and transition. I share with C. S. Lewis what some might consider to be a shocking and destructive habit of entering into dialogue with authors by underlining choice sentences in their books and entering my own comments (sometimes appreciative, sometimes critical) in their margins. Those annotations and disfigurements are marks of critical engagement and assimilation, a testimony to my reading of the text and an indication of how I reacted to what I encountered. On reading a text, I can see what grasped my attention, what questions were raised, and, occasionally, a new line of thought that emerged from this sustained interrogation of the text. (Lewis would often read texts multiple times, using different colors of ink to distinguish his comments on each reading.)

When working on old books from the seventeenth and eighteenth centuries in Oxford's Bodleian Library, I often found passages marked by previous readers of those bygone ages, who had underlined them or drawn lines or pointing fingers in the margins, highlighting what those long-dead readers had found and valued in the texts. The physical reality of a book can thus serve as a testimony to the value of the text and the engagement of its readers. Marginal annotations signal what C. S. Lewis's close friend Neville Coghill once termed a "continuous intoxication of discovery,"[10] by which he meant that a reader's mental horizons are expanded and enriched through close reading of a text. I can find physical and mental pleasure in handling old books, imagining who read them before me and wondering what they found within their pages. Why did they underline that word or phrase? What process of reflection lies behind that cryptic marginal *nota bene*?

Recently, I published a study of the neglected Swiss theologian Emil Brunner.[11] Like several of my recent books, this represented the late outcome of about twenty-five years of study and reflection, which began when I studied Brunner during a research trip to the University of Zürich in 1986. I gradually built up a library of Brunner's published works for close reading and annotation and slowly worked through them all, trying to absorb and make sense of the development of his thought. One of those books proved frustratingly difficult to acquire: his 1930 work *Gott und Mensch*, a collection of four essays on theological aspects of personal existence. In late 2012, I finally found a secondhand copy listed in the stocks of a Swiss bookseller and promptly ordered it. It arrived a few days later and I unwrapped it with much pleasure and anticipation, looking forward especially to reading its essay on "biblical psychology."

I opened the book, to find the name of the previous owner of the work inscribed on its title page. It was Brevard Childs (1923–2007), professor of Old Testament at Yale University from 1958 until 1999, considered by many (including myself) to be one of the most influential biblical scholars of the twentieth century. I found myself overwhelmed at the thought of holding and reading a book that the founder of canonical criticism had held and read before me. It reminded me that I was part of a great tradition of wrestling with Scripture and the reality of God that included such giants as Brunner and Childs. My pleasure in reading the text was thus both deferred and enhanced. I did indeed read the book later, and with great profit, but my most powerful and emotive memory of that reading was not so much what I had read but the thought of who had read it before me.

Let me make another observation. In reading a book, I force myself to read it in its totality. I may be looking for something specific—such as the discussion of a specific idea, the exploration of the meaning of a word, or a reference to an individual. Now, some might say that this is a mark of someone who urgently needs to discover the tools of modern scholarship. Why read works in their entirety when all an intelligent reader needs to do is use the "search" function to find any relevant passages in an electronic version of the text quickly and painlessly?

One obvious answer is that I might indeed be a kind of intellectual dinosaur, whose ossified research techniques reflect the conditions of the 1970s, which is when I began the serious business of research. Now, I have to admit that this is probably true, yet I still want to suggest that we recognize the weaknesses of this increasingly common practice of electronic searching. The discipline of reading books comprehensively and totally allows me to grasp their inner logic, to enter into the mind of the author in a way that is simply impossible if I were to limit myself to searching for individual words or phrases. This electronic process may be quick and easy, but it is also shallow and superficial, evading the critical process of intellectual inhabitation of a text that is the hallmark of serious scholarship.

Whether I am reading C. S. Lewis or Emil Brunner, I feel myself called on as a scholar to read them properly, carefully, and fully. Grasping the "big picture"—whether explicit or implicit—in someone's writings demands reading them closely and completely. I am conscious of my obligation as a scholar to give them due consideration and attention, knowing that a close reading of any worthwhile book will deliver its intellectual and spiritual rewards. Even when reading someone who I know I will end up criticizing—such as Richard Dawkins—I still take care to read his works in their totality, not making myself dependent on the kind of disembodied and decontextualized textual snippets that now circulate on the internet.

Finally, I have come to realize the importance of what I can only describe as serendipity—an unexpected discovery of a wonderful turn of phrase or a refreshingly different idea that I had not set out to explore. It happens to me regularly when browsing university library shelves, looking for a specific book, only to discover that the one next to it on the shelf (which is usually unknown to me) turns out to be far more interesting and engaging, opening up new and unexpected approaches to the same topic. Recent studies of creativity have highlighted the importance of such "accidental" discoveries and have argued for the need to enhance our capacity to be taken by surprise by these gracious moments of disclosure. As Pek van Andel and Danièle Bourcier recently suggested, we need to cultivate our capacities to remove blinders (*l'art d'enlever des oeillères*),[12] maximizing the possibilities for new discovery and insight. The physical realities of books are like treasure troves, waiting to be found in libraries—or in the Regent College bookshop!

~~~~~~~~~~

And so I finally turn from the praise of books to those who run bookshops. It is very possible to emphasize the importance of books while overlooking the means by which these find their way into our hands. Let me go back to that rather splendid quote from Francis Bacon with which I opened this chapter, in which he confessed his pleasure in finding "old wine to drink." The manager of a bookshop is like a good sommelier, who can recommend books—recent or vintage—that match their readers' needs, stretch their minds, and nourish their souls.

Earlier in this chapter, I reflected on my own experience of encountering books that I never knew about, stacked on shelves alongside more familiar works, awaiting my accidental discovery. What, though, if I had a guide—someone wiser and more informed—who would accompany me on my journey of exploration and discovery, reaching over my shoulder as I browsed, whispering, "Look at that one! You'll enjoy it!" The best bookseller is someone who loves books and knows which ones can be recommended. That's why I take such pleasure in honoring Bill. There are so few like him, just as there are so few theological bookshops that can compare to the one at Regent College.

If I were to end on a more somber note, I might express concern about the future of the publishing industry and, in particular, the radical changes that we have seen in the world of religious publishing in the last two decades, as so many familiar Christian publishing houses have merged or disappeared. Yet we need to remember that we live in a changing world, in which we have experienced seismic shifts in so many things, including the ways in which we access texts, the ways in which we read them, and the changing technologies by means of which they are produced. Perhaps medieval manuscript copyists were alarmed at Johannes Gutenberg's new printing press, fearing it might create havoc with their livelihoods and callings. Yet change always has an upside, as well as a downside, and we too easily focus on our fears and fail to see the opportunities that accompany these changes.

I do not know what the future of religious publishing will be, but I do know the importance of the "life of the mind"—the expansion of our vision of God and our need to grasp more firmly and fully the realities of the Christian faith. We need to be able to tap into the wisdom of others—past and present—who have the potential to inform, encourage, inspire, and challenge us. I suspect that printed books will continue to be with us for a long time to come, but whatever the future will hold, we need people like Bill who can point others to the rich pastures of Christian writing that have sustained so many in the past, and I believe will do so in the future as well. Bill has been, for many, a gateway to the wisdom of faith, and I take the greatest pleasure in honoring him and the sapiential role he has played for so many—including myself.

5

The Balcony and the Road

*A Framework for Understanding
Christian Discipleship*

Discipleship is an integral part of the Christian life. In this chapter, I want to reflect on the way we think about—or, better, how we imagine—this process of growing in the Christian faith. What framework is helpful as we reflect on how we might deepen our own faith and help others to do so as well?

I came across some words of the English church leader and theologian William Temple some years ago that have helped me to think about this important question: "Faith is not only the assent of our minds to doctrinal propositions: it is the commitment of our whole selves into the hands of a faithful Creator and merciful Redeemer."[1] Temple here highlights two of the fundamental elements of faith: grasping and exploring core Christian beliefs, and enhancing and deepening our personal commitment to God and Christ. We are called to think about our faith and absorb its living realities, so that

Based on a talk given to Christian academics at Hong Kong University on November 5, 2017.

they become part of our being. This, I think, is what the Danish philosopher Søren Kierkegaard meant when he spoke of an "appropriation process of the most passionate inwardness."[2] We need to *inhabit* the truth of the Christian faith, not see it as if we were external observers, viewing it disinterestedly from outside.

~~~~~~~

So what way of seeing the Christian life might we use to help us to think about this process of growing in our faith? I want to begin by reflecting on the framework developed by the theologian John Mackay (1889–1983) while he was president of Princeton Theological Seminary, which focuses on two core images—the balcony and the road. Mackay set this out in his *Preface to Christian Theology* (1941), in which he tried to recapture the significance of Christian theology in terms of "bringing back meaning into life" and "restoring the foundations upon which all true life and thought are built."[3] The context, of course, is the Second World War, which shattered human dreams of a "new age."

Mackay suggests that we, like those first disciples of Christ, find ourselves on the "road to Emmaus." We yearn to "listen to a Voice from beyond and catch the outline of a Face."[4] We are on a journey through a hostile world, struggling to progress either in reaching our goal or becoming better and deeper people as we travel. If we are to grow in our faith, Mackay argues, we need to see ourselves and our journey of faith from an "appropriate perspective." For Mackay, there are two perspectives that human beings bring to the business of trying to make sense of life and live meaningfully within the world. Mackay designates one "the balcony" and the other "the road,"[5] seeing both as symbols of the "state of the soul."

To understand Mackay's choice of these two "symbols" for these quite distinct attitudes to the quest for meaning in life, we need to reflect on his background. Mackay had a long interest in Christianity in Latin America,[6] and had learned Spanish in Madrid in 1915 to enable him to work as a missionary in Peru. While staying in Madrid, Mackay noticed that Spanish families often gathered on a balcony to look at the bustle of the street below. The balcony, he explained, was a "little platform in wood or stone that protrudes from the upper window of a Spanish home," from which the observers can watch all that happens on the street below. The balcony thus represents an observation point that is at some distance from what is being observed.[7]

Mackay contrasted this kind of detached "balconized existence" with life on the road below. "By the Road, I mean the place where life is tensely lived, where thought has its birth in conflict and concern, where choices are made and decisions are carried out."[8] For Mackay, the church and individual believers live out a pilgrim life on the road. The Christian is not a lone traveler but, rather, is part of a "fellowship of the Road," which seeks and hopes to find truth and meaning: "Truth is found upon the Road."[9]

Mackay's point is that Christian discipleship happens on the road. The balcony is an idealization, an intellectual aspiration that can never be achieved in practice. It is an "ivory tower," beloved of armchair philosophers. Philosophers of the past may have believed it was possible to take a God's-eye perspective and see all things clearly and distinctly, yet we now realize that we cannot extricate ourselves from the historical process. We cannot stand above and beyond it, so that we can see where it is going and judge our place within it. We have to figure things out from within the historical process itself.

For Mackay, Christians have their existence on the road and must come to realize and accept the limits that this places on their grasp and vision of reality. They cannot see the "big picture" of reality, in that their horizon limits what can be seen. They may yearn to stand on the balcony and see that "big picture"; that option, however, is simply not available to them. We are journeying on the road, seeking a knowledge that will illuminate our situation as we travel and help us become better people as we do so. For Mackay, there can be "no true knowledge of ultimate things" unless this arises from a concern and is "perfected in a commitment."[10] This leads to a set of questions emerging from the Christian life that might be described as practical rather than theoretical—questions such as, "How can I become what I ought to be? How can I know God? How can I relate to the purpose of the universe? How can we make the world a better place?" The believer is a wayfarer—someone who is on the road and knows there is no possibility of rising above that road.

I have long found this framework helpful in thinking about Christian discipleship. Mackay encourages me to think of growth in faith in terms of the accumulation of wisdom that will help sustain me as I travel along that road and try—to the limited extent possible within the conditions of this life, even through divine grace—to make myself a better person and the world a better place. Mackay captures the tragedy of the human epistemic situation with elegance, inviting us to realize the limits of our situation and appreciate that our puzzling and complex world is best illuminated by divine revelation rather than analyzed by human reason.

Yet Mackay's framework is helpful for another reason: it creates conceptual space for spiritual mentors, who, I have learned, are integral to the process of Christian discipleship. A mentor is someone who journeys alongside us on the road and shares the wisdom that he or she has gathered along the way. A mentor is not someone who stands on a fictional balcony, dispensing alleged wisdom from on high. Rather, mentors are part of the pilgrim community of faith, sharing the wisdom they have gained on the journey with those who accompany them on the road. Discipleship is about finding someone a few steps in front of us on the road and following that person. Mentors are usually—though not exclusively—older people who share their wisdom with those who are younger. So let me turn now to thinking about this notion of a mentor in more detail.

One of the most engaging French religious writers is François Fénelon (1651–1715), a Catholic archbishop, theologian, and poet. Although I have gained much from reading his "spiritual letters," his best-known work is *The Adventures of Telemachus*, first published anonymously in 1699.[11] This widely read work was a thinly veiled criticism of the autocratic rule of the "Sun King," Louis XIV, who promptly banished Fénelon from his court at Versailles, confining him to his diocese of Cambrai in northeastern France. The book takes the form of an imaginative exploration and expansion of a passage in Homer's *Odyssey* that recounts the education and formation of Telemachus, son of Odysseus and Penelope, who is accompanied by his tutor, Mentor, on his educational travels.

Where Homer presents Mentor as a somewhat ineffectual old man, Fénelon playfully represents this as a mere outward appearance masking a deep intelligence arising from his true identity as Minerva, the goddess of wisdom, in disguise. Mentor, for Fénelon, is the embodiment of wisdom and reflection—an older person who has internalized his learning and is willing to pass on that wisdom to younger people, such as Telemachus. For Fénelon, Mentor was someone who had accumulated wisdom over an extended period of time and acted as a source of wisdom, insight, and encouragement for Telemachus as he accompanied the younger man on his journeys of exploration and discovery. Mentor did not teach Telemachus specific skills but, rather, helped him to grow as a reflective and humane person. Mentor thus shaped the character of the younger man by challenging him to think differently, opening his eyes and mind to different perspectives.

This idea of the intergenerational transmission of wisdom remains important and needs to be distinguished from the notion of "coaching," in which those with certain competencies aim to transfer this to those under their care. Today, the term "mentor" has largely lost its associations with Homer and Fénelon and is often simply equated with a coach. Few now know that Mentor was a literary character and assume that the word "mentor" merely designates someone who functions as a teacher of certain skills.

Some Christians are concerned that the idea of a mentor has its origins in a secular culture and thus lacks a Christian history of use, yet Fénelon was deeply concerned with the intergenerational transmission of Christian wisdom and—unlike Homer—presented Mentor as playing an exemplary role in this process. Fénelon subtly contrasts the inexperience and naivety of the young Telemachus with the wisdom of the older Mentor, showing how Mentor's conversations with Telemachus as they journeyed together helped the younger person to develop virtue and insight along the road.

So how does this concept of mentoring, as Fénelon develops it, help the process of growing in faith and wisdom that we know as "Christian discipleship"? Let me share something of my own experience.

~~~~~~~~

After discovering Christianity in 1971, I found myself struggling to understand what I had embraced. My difficulties as a novice Christian disciple did not lie only in making sense of the basic ideas of faith as these were set out in the creeds. I was someone who loved the natural sciences and had once believed that the sciences and religious faith were locked into a conflict that made it impossible for a real scientist to be a religious believer. I was unsure where my journey of faith would take me. Would it force me to compartmentalize my mind, allocating separate regions of it to science and faith, so that I could avoid thinking about their potentially irreconcilable tensions? Were there other intellectual options, at that point unknown to me, that could allow me to see science and faith as aspects of a greater whole? Who could point me to these options—or, even better, tell me about them?

Although there were many Christian students at Oxford working in the field of the natural sciences, most adopted an approach that I valued but found difficult to work out in practice. All truth is God's truth, I was told. For this reason, scientific truth could not be inconsistent with the truths of the Christian faith. There might seem to be tensions between science and faith, but these were more apparent than real. At one level, I could see the merits in this approach, yet it seemed to me to be frustratingly abstract and generalized. I felt that I needed more help than this.

In the end, my difficulties were resolved through an imaginative leap, brought about by an older and wiser person who shared his own way of thinking with me. Charles A. Coulson, Oxford University's first professor of theoretical chemistry, was a Fellow of Wadham College, where I was an undergraduate. A year or so after my conversion, I heard Coulson—a prominent Methodist lay preacher—preach in Wadham Chapel on the fundamental coherence of nature and faith. The intellectual framework he outlined in his sermon provided a radical clarification of the issues and allowed me to see a way ahead. I was able to talk to him afterward about his ideas concerning the coherence of science and faith.[12] These remain integral to my thinking to this day.

Coulson became a mentor to me. Knowing that my specialist subject was quantum theory, he invited me to attend the annual conferences he organized on this subject at Wadham College, which exposed me to some of the latest thinking in the field. One of his core themes was that the idea of a "god of the gaps" was to be rejected. In its place, Coulson affirmed a Christian "big picture"— the articulation of a luminous vision of reality that offered insight into the scientific process and its successes, while at the same time setting out a larger narrative that allowed engagement with questions raised by science, yet lying beyond its capacity to answer. That notion of a "big picture" stands at the heart of my own thinking about the Christian faith and informs my research and writing to this day.

So would I have discovered such an approach without Coulson? Perhaps. Coulson, however, helped me to do more than understand his ideas; he embodied his own way of thinking. It had become part of him, shaping his attitudes toward science and faith. A few years back, I read a biography of the American physicist J. Robert Oppenheimer (1904–67), now remembered mainly as the "father of the atomic bomb." One of Oppenheimer's throwaway remarks has stayed with me: "The best way to send information is to wrap it up in a person."[13] Without people who are shaped by them, ideas remain abstract. To grasp the significance of an idea, we need to see what difference it makes to the way someone thinks, acts, and sees the world.

A mentor is not an authority figure but a person we come to respect and trust. Spiritually, we need people who can model for us what loving God and loving others actually looks like. Intellectually, we need people who have developed outlooks and practices that reflect their fundamental beliefs. Discipleship is better seen as a journey than something that happens in a classroom. It takes place *relationally* on the road, through observation, imitation, learning from mistakes, and the formation of habits and skills; it takes place *intellectually* on that same road, through collaboration and a sharing of practices with our fellow travelers, as we listen to how they understand the Bible, assimilate its ideas, and cope with the uncertainties of life.

Like any good mentor, Coulson embodied what he believed so that I could grasp the significance of his ideas through knowing him as a person. He died of cancer in 1974, so I never got to know him as well as I would have liked, but even our brief acquaintance was enough to help me grasp and then inhabit his way of seeing the relation of science and faith. The idea was *expressed* in his books, yet it was *embodied* in his life. Perhaps I was like an apprentice to a master, learning through both watching and listening.[14]

That's one of the reasons I enjoy reading (and sometimes even writing) biographies of people such as C. S. Lewis and other Christian luminaries. They help me to understand how theological ideas shape our lives through a process of reflective inhabitation. Such writers have journeyed on the road and passed their wisdom down to me. They challenge my judgments, constantly inviting me to see things in a new way and try out fresh approaches.

There are, of course, some people I would have loved to have known as mentors. Sadly, I shall never be able to know great writers of the past, such as Augustine of Hippo, Athanasius of Alexandria, or Martin Luther—to name only three individuals—or to journey alongside them in person and talk to them about their habits of thought, prayer, and adoration. Yet I can read their books. While this is no substitute for the living presence of a mentor, it allows me to absorb their ideas and work out how I might benefit from their wisdom. Though dead, they still speak to us, offering us encouragement and stimulus.

I now see books as providing a special category of mentoring, with a significant capacity to change and enrich our lives. I gladly acknowledge the importance of conversations with significant individuals in my early stages of faith. Yet, while my early conversations with Coulson opened up new ways of thinking, it was my subsequent engagement with his books that consolidated those ideas, adding breadth and depth to my new mental map of reality.[15] As I grow older, I find myself relying more on books than I did, partly because my own growth in faith more recently has not taken the form of acquiring new ideas but of deepening my appreciation of ones that I already knew by reading more about them and the words of other wayfarers on the road about how they understood and applied those ideas.

In closing, let me return to the framework I set out at the beginning of this chapter—the balcony and the road. All of us are on that road, even if we might wistfully dream of being on the balcony. We journey along that road in company, however, developing relationships of trust in which we encourage and gently challenge each other as we travel. We are wayfarers on our way to the New Jerusalem, finding ourselves motivated to continue by the thought of finally reaching our destination. Yet we can also use the journey wisely, seeing this as a time of preparation, during which we acquire habits of thought and action that emerge from the Christian "big picture."

Part of the process of discipleship is the expansion of our minds and souls that arises from a deeper understanding of the Christian faith, stimulated and enlarged by conversations with other wayfarers along the road and the books that have emerged from those journeys. The process of discipleship is nourished by the sharing of wisdom and acquired experience within the wandering people of God, who come to see their journey as a process of personal and spiritual growth.

We are also accompanied by our living and loving God, who does not stand above and beyond us as a distant spectator but travels with us in sorrow and joy, even when we pass through life's darker moments. This insight is solidified in the Christian doctrine of the incarnation, which speaks of Jesus Christ as God incarnate, present with us, even to the end of time, as we journey through this world. As I began this chapter by referring to Mackay's *Preface to Christian Theology*, let me close with its final words: "If the Road to Emmaus is still our road, the great Companion, who trod it then, treads it still, to lead the pilgrims of this twilight hour into the glory of a new dawn."[16] As Mackay reminds us, we do not merely journey with others; we journey in hope—a hope that, by God's grace, we shall one day be in a better place and have, by then, become better people.

PART 2

Growing in Wisdom

Four Practitioners

6

The Creative Mind

*Dorothy L. Sayers on Making Sense
of Our World*

O ne of the most distinctive features of human nature is our
innate yearning to try to make sense of the strange and
puzzling world we see around us. We find this desire to
understand and explain in the natural sciences, which set out to
make sense of the working of the natural world. This can be seen in
their emphasis on intelligibility, expressed in the scientific quest to
make accounting for natural phenomena logically coherent.[1] Yet this
emphasis on making sense of things is found far beyond the realms
of the natural sciences. It is found, for example, in Christianity—
not, perhaps, as its dominant theme but certainly as an important
aspect of its overall vision of reality. Exploring and applying this
aspect of Christian faith is, in my view, an integral aspect of the
discipleship of the mind.

Based on a public lecture given at Gresham College, London, on November 29,
2016.

The philosopher Keith Yandell offers a good account of this aspect of faith: "A religion is a conceptual system that provides an interpretation of the world and the place of human beings in it, bases an account of how life should be lived given that interpretation, and expresses this interpretation and lifestyle in a set of rituals, institutions and practices."[2]

Perhaps the same point is made more forcefully by psychologists of religion, who stress the importance of religion in the human making of meaning.[3] Religion can provide a comprehensive and integrated framework of meaning that helps to explain our experiences and situations, while providing a way of helping individuals transcend their own experience and connect up with something greater.[4]

There is, of course, more to making sense of reality than simply offering an explanation of things. What of the related notion of coherence, for example, which concerns how things are related to and interconnected with each other? Many would link this pursuit of coherence with a specifically religious agenda: "This is our first demand of religion—that it should illumine life and make it a whole."[5]

So how do we make sense of things? For the scientist, one of the most important general approaches is that of induction—the generalization from specific examples, in which universal patterns are discerned on the basis of empirical observation. From such observations we generate more general and universal ways of understanding our world, which are expressed in theories and hypotheses.

Charles Peirce, the great American pragmatist philosopher of the nineteenth century, argued that the fundamental principle of scientific thinking was the process he called "abduction"—namely, the attempt to find an intellectual pattern that made sense of what was observed, even if this pattern was not itself disclosed by those observations. Abduction is a kind of nondeductive inference that can be thought of as "the process of forming explanatory hypotheses." Perhaps most importantly, Peirce argued that this process is a "logical operation" that introduces a "new idea"—an idea that seems to connect up all the observations to disclose a pattern rather than just a random collection of facts.[6]

Peirce invites us to generate theories and explanations, then test them to find out how well they seem to accommodate the evidence. Abduction is the "provisional adoption of an explanatory hypothesis"—an intellectual strategy for generating ideas, explanations, and theories; we then have to confirm the theory by checking it out against observation.[7] As Peirce understands it, abduction is thus a kind of "search strategy" that leads us to generate some "promising explanatory conjecture which is then subject to further test."[8] For Peirce, the best example of this kind of thinking is found in the natural sciences. Yet the same pattern of thought can be found elsewhere—as in medical diagnosis and detective fiction.[9] Our observations are essentially clues to the deeper meaning or inner workings of our world.

All of this helps us to understand why we like detective novels so much. Writers such as Sir Arthur Conan Doyle, Agatha Christie, Raymond Chandler, and Dorothy L. Sayers built their reputations on being able to hold their readers' interest as countless mysterious murder cases were solved before their eyes. We devour the cases of fictional detectives such as Sherlock Holmes, Philip Marlowe, Lord Peter Wimsey, and Miss Jane Marple. These writers skillfully assemble a body of evidence and a series of observations, and challenge us to find the hidden pattern that makes sense of them.

Dorothy L. Sayers (1893–1957) was one of the most widely read authors of the "Golden Age" of British crime fiction, before developing her interest in Christian theology. Sayers saw human beings as searching for "patterns" in life and explored this theme in her Peter Wimsey detective novels as well as her religious writings. How can we find the best explanation of what we observe? Sayers was a shrewd analyst of the complexity of life and offers a rich and nuanced account of why human beings attach so much importance to discerning meaning in life and why we enjoy solving puzzles—whether this relates to the identity of the murderer in *Gaudy Night* or "ultimate questions," such as, What is the meaning of life?

Sayers saw her detective novels as being about discerning a pattern within events that pointed to the way in which an intellectual puzzle could be solved. She developed this theme in a lecture that she proposed to broadcast to the French nation in early 1940, to bolster their morale in the early stages of the Second World War, by emphasizing the importance of France as a source of great literary detectives. Unfortunately, Sayers's talk celebrating the French literary detective was never transmitted to what would doubtless have been an appreciative French public. Paris fell to invading German armies shortly before she was scheduled to speak. Happily, however, the text has survived.

One of the central themes of Sayers's lecture is that detective fiction appeals to our deep yearning to make sense of what seems to some to be an unrelated series of events. Within those events, however, are the clues, the markers of significance, that can lead to the solution of the mystery. We "follow, step by step, Ariadne's thread, and finally arrive at the center of the labyrinth."[10] We need to pause here and focus on the central image of Sayers's analogy. Steeped in a classical education, Sayers drew on the ancient Greek legend of Minos, king of Crete, who instructed the great architect Daedalus to build a labyrinth near his palace at Knossos to house the Minotaur—a hybrid of a man and a bull. The labyrinth was famously complicated. Once inside its dark passages, it proved impossible for anyone to find the way back out again. Those unfortunate enough to enter were thus doomed to being eaten by the Minotaur. It was just a matter of time.

Having conquered the city of Athens, Minos demanded that every year Athens would send seven maidens and seven youths, as a tribute, to be devoured by the Minotaur. Theseus, son of Aegeus, king of Athens, volunteered to join the band of youths who were to be sent to Crete to be sacrificed. Ariadne, daughter of Minos, fell in love with him and offered to help him conquer the labyrinth and kill the Minotaur if he would marry her and take her away from Crete. He agreed—although, of course, in the end he failed to make good on his promise. Trusting him, Ariadne gave Theseus a ball of red thread, which he unrolled as he entered the labyrinth. Having found and killed the Minotaur, Theseus was able to find his way out of the labyrinth by following the thread back to its source. Ariadne's thread was the key to finding the way through a dark and confusing structure. Sayers realized how this potent image could be used as an analogy for the intellectual framework within which a detective novel is set.

Sayers, like so many before her, appreciated that the detective novel appeals to our implicit belief in the intrinsic rationality of the world around us and our ability to discover its deeper patterns. Something important or interesting has taken place—such as the mysterious death of Sir Charles Baskerville—but what *really* happened? We were not there to observe this event, yet by careful analysis of clues, we may identify the most likely explanation of what actually took place. The image of Ariadne's thread thus reappears, in the form of a thread of an argument—a way of linking together a series of events or observations so that we can see their underlying pattern. To use an image popularized by the great British philosopher of science William Whewell (1794–1866), we must find the best thread on which to string the pearls of our observations, so that they disclose their true pattern: "The facts are known but they are insulated and unconnected. . . . The pearls are there but they will not hang together until someone provides the string."[11]

Sayers's detective novels can be seen as a literary application of what is now known in the philosophy of science as "inference to the best explanation." For every set of observations, there are several competing explanations. So which of these is the best? Which thread best connects and displays the pearls of our observations?

What criteria might be used to make this evaluation? We can see this process of reflection in Sayers's novel *The Unpleasantness at the Bellona Club*, set in London's high society during the 1920s. Sayers opens the chapter describing Lord Peter Wimsey's breakthrough in the mystery surrounding the curious death of General Fentiman by reflecting on the criteria that might be used in choosing one theory over another:

> "What put you on to this poison business?" [Detective Inspector Parker] asked.
>
> "Aristotle, chiefly," replied Wimsey. "He says, you know, that one should always prefer the probable impossible to the improbable possible. It was possible, of course, that the General should have died off in that neat way at the most confusing moment. But how much nicer and more probable that the whole thing had been stage-managed."[12]

While some professional philosophers might wince at Sayers's appeal to Aristotle, her point is perfectly reasonable.[13] Once Wimsey had found this pattern, he was able to superimpose it on the otherwise puzzling series of events at the Bellona Club and show how these threads were woven together in his intellectual solution, disclosing a pattern that linked what would otherwise have seemed to be disconnected events.

At points, Sayers's critics felt that her detective novels displayed an excessive concern for the discernment of abstract patterns rather than exploring the complexity of human motivations and ambitions. Raymond Chandler, for example, felt that Sayers had become absorbed with the issue of "logic and deduction," so that the "artificial pattern required by the plot" came to overwhelm the plausibility of her characters, in effect forcing them to do some "unreal things" in order to fit this template.[14] Sayers herself later came to appreciate such concerns, expressing misgivings about the tendency to see detective fiction simply as a deductive assault on a set of data, ignoring issues of human character and the ambiguous status of evidence.[15]

For Sayers, life was also to be seen as a quest for a pattern of meaning. She was convinced that Christianity gave her a tool by which she might "make sense of the universe," disclosing hidden patterns and allowing meaning to be discerned within its otherwise opaque mysteries. If *The Nine Tailors* addressed the mysteries of the universe, *Gaudy Night* engaged the mysteries of the human heart.[16] Her partly autobiographical work, *Cat O'Mary*, makes reference to this quest for meaning and the intellectual pleasure it brought to its central character, Katherine: "When Katherine sat down to prepare a passage of Molière, she experienced the actual physical satisfaction of plaiting and weaving together innumerable threads to make a pattern, a tapestry, a created beauty."[17]

Sayers came to believe that such patterns were not human inventions, but represented a pattern of the creative mind,[18] itself echoing the deeper patterns of divine rationality. Sayers prized the rationalizing capacity of Christianity so greatly that she occasionally wondered if she had actually fallen in love with its intellectual patterns rather than its content—above all, the historical figure of Jesus Christ. Perhaps the work that deals with this theme in greatest detail is her classic work *The Mind of the Maker* (1941).

Sayers was not a professional theologian; however, it is clear that her *Mind of the Maker* is essentially an outworking of her own distinct notion of the "image of God" in humanity as a kind of imaginative template, which predisposes human beings to think and imagine in certain ways.[19] The "same pattern of the creative mind" is evident in both theology and art, and points to a deeper inbuilt imaginative template that enables and encourages human beings to discern patterns in the deepest aspects of life. Sayers was inclined to think that the pattern of human creative processes "correspond[s] to the actual structure of the living universe," so that the "pattern of the creative mind" is an "eternal Idea" rooted in the being of God.

If we conclude that the creative mind is in fact the very grain of the spiritual universe, we cannot arbitrarily stop our investigations with the man who happens to work in stone, or paint, or music, or letters. We shall have to ask ourselves whether the same pattern is not also exhibited in the spiritual structure of every man and woman. And, if it is, whether, by confining the average man and woman to uncreative activities and an uncreative outlook, we are not doing violence to the very structure of our being.[20]

Sayers thus leads us into one of the most important discussions of our time—the question of the rationality of our beliefs, whether these are religious, moral, political, or secular. For Sayers, Christianity was a discovery of the way things really are, not an invention of the way we would like things to be. The philosopher Ludwig Wittgenstein realized that meaning and happiness arise when we believe that we are thinking and living in accordance with something deeper and greater than ourselves: "In order to live happily I must be in agreement with the world. And that is what 'being happy' means."[21] We need to grasp the "big picture" of the universe and position ourselves within it.

Yet we seem unable to grasp this full picture by ourselves. We need help if we are to see beyond the tantalizing limits imposed on us by being human. This is, of course, a classic theme in Christian theology. The notion of divine revelation is about the disclosure of a view of reality that we did not invent and that lies beyond the capacity of human reason to grasp fully. Revelation is not about the violation of human reason, but a demonstration of its limits and a disclosure of what lies tantalizingly beyond its limits. It is about the illumination of the landscape of our world, so that we can see things more clearly. For Christians, this capacity to see things as they really are—rather than as they are glimpsed from the surface—is a gracious gift of God. Our eyes need to be opened so that what we once deemed to be an incoherence is recognized as arising out of our inability to see fully and properly.

For Christian writers such as Sayers, religious faith is not a rebellion against reason, but a revolt against the imprisonment of humanity within the cold walls of a rationalist dogmatism. Logic and facts can only "take us so far; then we have to go the rest of the way toward belief."[22] Human logic may be rationally adequate, but it is also existentially deficient. Faith declares that there is more to life than this. It doesn't contradict reason but transcends it. It elicits and invites rational consent, but does not compel it. Sadly, some of those who boast that they are "freethinkers" are simply imprisoned by a defunct eighteenth-century rationalism, unaware of the radical changes in our understanding of rationality that have emerged in the last fifty years.[23]

So how does Sayers work out her approach in relation to her Christian faith? How does this play into her vision of Christianity being embraced by and enfolded within the "creative mind"? Sayers argues that we need to appreciate the importance of theology and explore how this affects the ways that we think and behave. She made this point with particular force in her lecture "Creed or Chaos?," given during the depths of the Second World War. Many were then worried about the threat to traditional moral values posed by the rise of Nazism and the rapid military advance of German armies across Western Europe. Sayers argued that moral values ultimately reflect a dogma on which they depend for their credibility.

Some British intellectuals of that age, anxious to get rid of Christian ideas but keep its moral framework, had failed to realize that Christian values could not be sustained without the worldview on which they are based. Nazi beliefs gave rise to one set of moral values; Christian beliefs to another. Christian ethics depend on, and are an expression of, the Christian worldview. Sayers ridiculed secularists who were trying "to uphold a particular standard of ethical values which derives from Christian dogma" while at the same time trying to get rid of "the very dogma which is the sole rational foundation for those values."[24] In the end, Sayers thus declared, this real battle was not about moral values but the worldviews on which those values were based. Safeguarding Christian distinctiveness is the essential precondition for safeguarding Christian values.

For Sayers, the creeds set out Christianity's distinct vision of reality and remind Christians that, in the end, their lives and thoughts are shaped by this view. Without a creed, there would be moral chaos. A "doctrineless" Christianity is simply impossible, in that Christians need to think about the nature of their faith and its implications for the way they live. Sayers proved capable of summarizing some core Christian doctrines in surprisingly pithy and creative ways—such as her succinct account of the relevance of the doctrine of the incarnation: "If Christ was only a man, then he is entirely irrelevant to any thought about God; if he is only God, then he is entirely irrelevant to any experience of human life."[25] Yet, for many, her most interesting theological reflections concern the doctrine of the Trinity.

In *The Mind of the Maker*, Sayers explores some aspects of the doctrine of the Trinity by appealing to the "pattern of the creative mind."[26] Her experience as an author, Sayers declared, suggested that there are three distinct stages in the process of creative activity that underlies the writing of a book: the *idea* itself, its *implementation*, and the process of *interaction* with its readers. A book comes into existence initially as an ideal construct, built outside time and space but complete in the mind of the author. It is then realized in time and space, by pen, ink, and paper. The creation is only complete, however, when someone reads the book, thus interacting with the mind of its maker and being transformed by the author's vision.

The mind of the author thus leads initially to the act of writing, then the experience of reading and comprehending the story—but the process is only complete when the author's idea has entered into a reader's mind. There is a natural progression in what Sayers terms "Book as Thought," "Book as Written," and "Book as Read."[27] Sayers here identifies an explicit link between God's self-communication and the doctrine of the Trinity. God is the source of revelation, but that revelation takes place in a specific historical form and, thus, needs to be understood and interpreted by human thinkers.

Sayers's emphasis on our need to think about God is linked with her cautionary affirmation that human reason is simply not capable of a total comprehension of God. God will always prove resistant to human rationalization, precisely because the human mind cannot fully grasp the vastness of the divine. Sayers makes this important theological point using an analogy familiar to many of her readers. Trying to get God into a verbal formula is like trying to force a large and irritated cat into a small basket. As soon as you tuck in his head, his tail comes out. Once his back paws are inside, the front paws appear again. Even when you finally manage to squeeze the cat into the basket, his "dismal wailings" make it clear that "some essential dignity in the creature has been violated and a wrong done to its nature."[28]

Now Sayers's analogy is inadequate in many respects, but it nevertheless makes an important point: the inability of any human conceptual scheme to contain or control the living God. Christian theology has long recognized that it is impossible for us to represent or describe God adequately using human language. The sheer vastness of God causes human images and words to falter, if not break down completely, as they try to depict God fully and faithfully. That's why the theological notion of "mystery" is so important. A mystery is not something that is contradicted by reason but, rather, something that exceeds reason's capacity to discern and describe— thus transcending, rather than contradicting, reason. Sayers's analogy of the protesting captive cat reminds us that we must resist our natural human tendency to limit reality to what we can understand and, instead, open up our minds to a reality that is greater than our capacity to comprehend it. As the great Puritan writer Richard Baxter once remarked, we may well *know* God, but to *comprehend* God lies beyond our capacity.[29]

It is a fitting thought with which to end. Christian discipleship is not about mastering God, but being mastered by God—not as an act of craven intellectual submission to someone we fear, but as an act of joyful intellectual enrichment arising from the expansion of our rational and imaginative capacities in response to a captivating vision of God, which ends up setting us free. Perhaps it is fitting to end with a famous prayer often attributed to Augustine of Hippo that weaves these themes together so elegantly:

> Eternal God, you are the light of the minds who know you, the life of the souls who love you, and the strength of the souls who serve you. Help us to know you that we may truly love you, so to love you that we may fully serve you, whose service is perfect freedom.

7

C. S. Lewis on the Reasonableness of the Christian Faith

The fiftieth anniversary of the death of C. S. Lewis in 2013 has seen a new interest in his writings and increased discussion of his distinctive approach to thinking about the Christian faith. Lewis is now firmly established as one of the greatest Christian apologists of the twentieth century, with a continuing legacy of influence in the twenty-first. Few apologists have achieved anything approaching his impact, which transcends denominational barriers.

Lewis was born in Northern Ireland and was a layman of the Church of England. The decision to honor him at Westminster Abbey by dedicating a memorial to him in Poets' Corner is an important

An address given at Westminster Abbey on November 21, 2013, to mark the fiftieth anniversary of the death of C. S. Lewis and his installation in Poets' Corner. A shorter version of this lecture, rewritten for a more academic readership, was published as "An Enhanced Vision of Rationality: C. S. Lewis on the Reasonableness of Christian Faith," *Theology* 116, no. 6 (2013): 410–17. I am grateful to the editor of *Theology* for permission to reproduce some material from this earlier article.

reaffirmation of his cultural and religious identity, right at the heart of the British religious and political establishment. Lewis's genius is such that he is loved and valued far beyond the confines of the United Kingdom and the Church of England; yet, as the huge attendances at the recent anniversary events in the United Kingdom have made abundantly clear, Lewis is both remembered and admired here, in this nation and church.

Lewis also appeals to both fans and academics. If I might borrow a phrase from Gregory the Great (c. 540–604) in his commentary on the book of Job, Lewis's works are "like a river, both shallow and deep, in which a lamb may walk and an elephant swim." The point Gregory was making was that the Bible could be read and appreciated at multiple levels, popular and academic. That is most certainly true of Lewis! Lewis is read and loved by a wide readership, yet this anniversary year has marked an important transition, in that Lewis is now being regarded with increased seriousness by academics, especially at Oxford and Cambridge. Many of you will have read Rowan Williams's brilliant engagement with Narnia.[1] It is surely significant that one of the world's greatest theologians, a former archbishop of Canterbury who is now master of Lewis's old Cambridge college, takes such delight in Narnia and helps us find new depths of meaning within it.

This recognition of Lewis by the British religious establishment is long overdue. The foundations for this appreciation were laid as long ago as 1946, when the ancient Scottish University of St. Andrews awarded Lewis the honorary degree of doctor of divinity. Professor Donald Baillie, dean of the university's Faculty of Divinity, declared at the ceremony that Lewis had "succeeded in capturing the attention of many who will not readily listen to professional theologians," and had "arranged a new kind of marriage between theological reflection and poetic imagination."[2] The passing of time has confirmed that Baillie was right on both counts. Perhaps, to use a musical image, Lewis is better seen as an arranger than as a composer. But some of his theological "arrangements" and "variations on themes" seem to have captured the popular imagination where the originals did not.

So what is Lewis's approach to telling the truth and why has it been so successful? I am going to explore here Lewis's distinctive understanding of the rationality of faith, which emphasizes the reasonableness of Christianity without imprisoning it within an impersonal and austere rationalism.

Lewis himself was an atheist as a younger man,[3] convinced of the fundamental irrationality of faith and its incapacity to accommodate the brutality and senselessness of the Great War, in which he fought from 1917 to 1918. Yet Lewis's decision to limit himself to a rationalist worldview proved to be imaginatively sterile and uninteresting, leaving him existentially dissatisfied. It became clear to Lewis that pure reason offered him a bleak intellectual landscape that he could not bear to inhabit. Yet this, his reason insisted, was all that there was. To believe otherwise was pure fantasy. Lewis's imagination taught him that there had to be more: "Nearly all that I loved I believed to be imaginary; nearly all that I believed to be real I thought grim and meaningless."[4]

Lewis's study of English literature, especially the poetry of George Herbert, left him with gnawing doubts about his atheism. Herbert and others seemed able to connect up with a world that Lewis was tempted to dismiss as illusory, yet which haunted his imagination: "On the one side, a many-islanded sea of poetry and myth; on the other, a glib and shallow rationalism."[5] Might, Lewis wondered, the deepest intuitions of his imagination challenge the shallow truths of his dogmatic reason? And even triumph over it?

So how did Lewis break free from this rationalist prison? Lewis's understanding of the reasonableness of the Christian faith rests on a distinct way of grasping the rationality of the created order and its ultimate grounding in God. Where some favor deductive arguments for the existence of God, Lewis offers his own distinct approach, which is more inductive than deductive; more visual than purely rational.

Lewis's approach is difficult to simplify, as it is highly nuanced, but perhaps we could set out the key aspects of his approach as follows. The truths of the Christian faith lie beyond the reach of human reason; yet when those truths are presented and grasped, their rationality can easily be discerned. And one hallmark of that rationality is the ability of the Christian faith to make things intelligible.

It is clear that Lewis was drawn to Christianity because of both its intellectual capaciousness and its imaginative appeal. It made sense of things, without limiting itself to what could be understood or grasped by reason. Lewis, it seems to me, echoes a theme we find in the final canto of Dante's *Divine Comedy*, where the great Florentine poet and theologian expresses the idea that Christianity provides a vision of things—something wonderful that can be seen, yet proves resistant to verbal expression:

> From that moment onwards my power of sight exceeded
> That of speech, which fails at such a vision.[6]

For Lewis, there is always a sense of a "beyond," a "numinous"—something of enormous significance that lies beyond our reason, hinted at more by intuition than by logic. This point had been made earlier by G. K. Chesterton (who Lewis greatly admired). "Every true artist," Chesterton argued, feels "that he is touching transcendental truths; that his images are shadows of things seen through the veil."[7] While the intellectual capaciousness of the Christian faith can be rationally analyzed, Lewis hints that it is best imaginatively communicated.

Lewis invites us to see Christianity as offering us a standpoint (a Platonic *synoptikon*, if you like) from which we may survey things and grasp their intrinsic coherence and interconnectedness. We see how things connect together. Lewis consistently uses a remarkably wide range of visual metaphors—such as sun, light, blindness, and shadows—to help us understand the nature of a true understanding of things. Where some argue that rationality concerns the ability of reason to give an account of things, Lewis frames this more in terms of our ability to see their relationships. This has two highly significant consequences.

First, it means that Lewis sees reason and imagination as existing in a collaborative relationship. Reason without imagination is potentially dull and limited; imagination without reason is potentially delusory and escapist. Lewis develops a notion of "imagined"—not imaginary—reality, which is capable of being grasped by reason and visualized by the imagination.

Second, it means that Lewis makes extensive use of verbal illustrations or analogies, to enable us to see things in a new way. Lewis's famous apologetic for the doctrine of the Trinity in *Mere Christianity* suggests that our difficulties arise primarily because we fail to see it properly. If we see it another way—as, for example, an inhabitant of a two-dimensional world might try to grasp and describe the structure of a three-dimensional reality—then we begin to grasp its intrinsic rationality. Lewis's apologetic often takes the form of a visual invitation: try seeing it this way! The rationality of the Trinity needs to be shown, not proved—and it is shown by allowing us to see it in the right way.

Perhaps this helps us appreciate the special appeal of Lewis's Chronicles of Narnia, which present a way of seeing things, embodied within stories, that turns out to be rationally plausible and imaginatively attractive. Lewis's Oxford colleague Austin Farrer suggested that Lewis's apologetic approach might initially look like an argument, but on closer inspection, it turned out to be an encouragement to see things in a new way and, thus, grasp the rationality of faith. Lewis, Farrer suggested, makes us "think we are listening to an argument," when in reality "we are presented with a vision, and it is the vision that carries conviction."[8]

For example, consider Lewis's imaginative visualization of a theological truth—the entrapment of the human soul through sin—in

The Voyage of the "Dawn Treader." Lewis's opening line in this book is seen by many as one of its most memorable features: "There was a boy called Eustace Clarence Scrubb, and he almost deserved it." Eustace Scrubb is portrayed as a thoroughly unsympathetic character, whom Lewis develops as an example of selfishness. It's difficult to like him to begin with, and it's just as difficult to feel sorry for him when he changes into a dragon as a result of his "greedy, dragonish thoughts."⁹

The thoroughly obnoxious Eustace encounters some enchanted gold that he believes will make him the master of all! Instead, it masters him. Lewis loved old Norse mythology and borrowed the Norse story about the greedy giant Fáfnir, who turned himself into a dragon to protect his ill-won gain. So Eustace becomes a dragon. Lewis presents Eustace's initial transformation into a dragon and his subsequent "undragoning" as a double transformation that reveals both Eustace's selfish, fallen nature and the transforming power of divine grace.

The Voyage of the "Dawn Treader" provides a brilliant description of Eustace's realizing, to his horror, that he has become a dragon. He doesn't like this at all, and he frantically tries to scratch off his dragon's skin. Yet each layer he removes merely reveals yet another layer of scales beneath it. He simply cannot break free from his prison. He is trapped. So having become a dragon, how does Eustace stop being one? It seems to lie beyond his power to change himself into what he wants to be.

But salvation lies to hand. Aslan appears and tears away at the dragon flesh with his claws. And when the scales are finally removed, Aslan plunges the raw and bleeding Eustace into a well, from which he emerges purified and renewed, with his humanity restored. The story line is dramatic, realistic, and shocking, but the power of the narrative brings home the Christian themes that Lewis believed could not be described as effectively through a series of well-intentioned theological lectures. And while Lewis drew his dragon imagery from

Norse mythology, the story of the "undragoning" draws on the rich ideas and imagery of the New Testament.

What are we to learn from this powerful and shocking story, so realistically depicted? As the startlingly raw imagery of Aslan tearing at Eustace's flesh makes clear, Eustace has been trapped by forces over which he has no control. The one who would be master has instead been mastered. The dragon is a symbol not so much of sin itself as of the power of sin to entrap, captivate, and imprison. It can only be broken and mastered by the redeemer. Aslan is the one who heals and renews Eustace, restoring him to what he was intended to be.

The immersion in the water of the well is immediately familiar, picking up on the New Testament's language about baptism as dying to self and rising to Christ (Rom. 6). Eustace is tossed into the well by Aslan and emerges renewed and restored. (The omission of this aspect of the "undragoning" of Eustace in the recent movie version of *The Voyage of the "Dawn Treader"* was one of the more irritating and unnecessary of its many weaknesses.)

You see my point. Lewis takes a classic theological doctrine and transposes it into a narrative—a narrative that is embraced imaginatively, not simply rationally understood. He breathes new life into a traditional doctrine by inviting us to see it. We are shown what sin is all about, not merely told about it.

Although some have tried to force Lewis into a purely rationalist way of thinking, this does not do him justice. Lewis does not try to prove the existence of God on a priori grounds. Instead, he invites us to see how what we observe in the world around us and experience within us "fits" the Christian way of seeing things. Lewis often articulates this way of "seeing things" in terms of a "myth"—that is to say, a story about reality that both invites its "imaginative embrace" and communicates a conceptual framework, by which other things are to be seen.[10] The imagination embraces the narrative; reason consequently reflects on its contents.

So how does this approach to the reasonableness of faith work out in practice? Let's consider Lewis's celebrated "argument from desire," exploring both its rational structure and its apologetic appeal.

The starting point for Lewis's approach is a human experience—a longing for something undefined and possibly undefinable, that is as insatiable as it is elusive. Lewis sets out versions of this argument at several points in his writings, including the Chronicles of Narnia. In *Surprised by Joy*, Lewis described his childhood experiences of intense longing (which he names "Joy") for something unknown and elusive, triggered by such things as the fragrance of a flowering currant bush in the garden of his childhood home in Belfast or reading Henry Wadsworth Longfellow's poem in the style of the Swedish poet Esaias Tegnér. Lewis's epiphany of "Joy" bathed his everyday world of experience with beauty and wonder, but what did it mean—if it meant anything at all? What way of seeing it might help him to make sense of it? How was he to interpret it?

While an atheist, Lewis dismissed such experiences as illusory. Yet he became increasingly dissatisfied with such simplistic reductive explanations. His growing familiarity with what he termed the "Christian mythology"—Lewis here uses the term "myth" in the sense of a "narrated worldview"—led him to appreciate that these experiences could easily and naturally be accommodated within its explanatory framework. What if God were an active questing personal agent, as Christianity affirmed to be the case? If so, God could easily be understood as the "source from which those arrows of Joy had been shot at me ever since childhood."[11]

In the 1941 sermon "The Weight of Glory," Lewis develops this theme further by exploring the human quest for beauty. Lewis argues that this is really a search for the source of that beauty, which is mediated through the things of this world but not contained within them. "The books or the music in which we thought the beauty was located will betray us if we trust to them: it was not *in* them, it only came *through* them, and what came through them was longing."[12]

Without a Christian way of seeing things, this longing remains "uncertain of its object."[13] Its true goal remains to be identified and attained. Christianity, Lewis declares, gives us the intellectual framework that both interprets the experience and leads us to its true goal.

In *Mere Christianity*, Lewis sets out this approach in a somewhat different way, while still appealing to the elusiveness of our experiences of "Joy." The experiences he had in mind are shared across the human spectrum, often expressed in quotidian language as a sense of there being "something there." The great Russian novelist Fyodor Dostoyevsky, for example, in his story "The Dream of a Ridiculous Man," spoke of "a nostalgic yearning, bordering at times on unendurably poignant sorrow," which was experienced in "the dreams of my heart and in the reveries of my soul."[14] Bertrand Russell, one of the most articulate and influential British atheist writers of the twentieth century, put a similar thought into words as follows: "The centre of me is always and eternally a terrible pain . . . a searching for something beyond what the world contains, something transfigured and infinite—the beatific vision—God—I do not find it, I do not think it is to be found—but the love of it is my life. . . . It is the actual spring of life within me."[15]

Russell's daughter, Katharine Tait, recalled that he was contemptuous of organized religion, dismissing its ideas mainly because he disliked those who held them. Yet Tait took the view that her father's life was really an unacknowledged, perhaps disguised, search for God: "Somewhere at the back of my father's mind, at the bottom of his heart, in the depths of his soul, there was an empty space that had once been filled by God, and he never found anything else to put in it." Russell was now haunted by a "ghost-like feeling of not belonging in this world."[16]

These are the kinds of experience to which Lewis appeals—a sense of hovering on the brink of discovering something of immense significance, linked with a sense of sorrow and frustration when what seemed to be so close tantalizingly disappears beyond our reach. Like smoke, it cannot be clasped. As Lewis puts it, "There was something we grasped at, in that first moment of longing, which just fades away in the reality."[17] So what does this sense of unfulfilled longing mean? To what does it point?

Some, Lewis concedes, might suggest that this frustration arises from looking for its true object in the wrong places; others that, since further searching will only result in repeated disappointment, there is simply no point trying to find something better than the present world.

Yet Lewis suggests that there is a third approach, which recognizes that these earthly longings are "only a kind of copy, or echo, or mirage" of our true homeland. Since this overwhelming desire cannot be fulfilled through anything in the present world, this suggests that its ultimate object lies beyond the present world: "If I find in myself a desire which no experience in this world can satisfy, the most probable explanation is that I was made for another world."

Here, as throughout his apologetic writings, the starting point of Lewis's approach does not lie with the Bible or the Christian tradition but with shared human experience and observation. How do we make sense of them? Lewis's genius as an apologist lay in his ability to show how a viewpoint derived from the Bible and the Christian tradition was able to offer a more satisfactory explanation of common human experience than its rivals—especially the atheism he had once himself espoused.

Lewis's apologetic approach is to identify a common human observation or experience, then show how it fits, naturally and plausibly, within a Christian way of looking at things.[18] For Lewis, Christianity provided a "big picture," an intellectually capacious and imaginatively satisfying way of seeing things. Lewis was always emphatic that nothing can be proved on the basis of observation or experience. Yet while such observations of nature or our own experiences prove nothing, they can suggest certain possibilities and even intimate what they might mean. That's what Lewis was trying to express when he wrote, "A true philosophy may sometimes validate an experience of nature; an experience of nature cannot validate a philosophy. Nature will not verify any theological or metaphysical proposition (or not in the manner we are now considering); she will help to show what it means."[19]

Lewis's approach could be framed like this: Christianity holds that the natural order—including our own reasoning—is shaped by the God who created all things. As Augustine of Hippo and Blaise Pascal had argued before him, Lewis affirms that the absence of God causes us to experience longing—a yearning for God, which we misinterpret as a longing for something located within the finite and created order. Conversion is thus partly about a semiotic transformation, in which we realize that something we believed to be pointing to one thing in fact points to something rather different.

We could set out Lewis's argument more formally as follows: We experience desires that no experience in this world seems able to satisfy. Yet Christianity tells us that we are made for another world. And when things are seen in this way, this sort of experience is exactly what we would expect. The appeal is not so much to cold logic as to intuition and imagination, resting on an imaginative dynamic of discovery. Lewis invites his audience to see their experiences through a set of Christian spectacles and notice how these bring what might otherwise be fuzzy or blurred into sharp focus. For Lewis, the ability of the Christian faith to accommodate our experience, naturally and easily, is an indicator of its truth. This is not really an argument at all; it is more about observing and affirming the fit between a theory and observation. It is like trying on a hat or shirt for size. How well does it fit? How many of our observations of the world can it accommodate and how persuasively? That's what Lewis's mentor G. K. Chesterton was also getting at when he remarked that "the phenomenon does not prove religion, but religion explains the phenomenon."[20]

The same approach is found in Lewis's "argument from morality." This is sometimes portrayed in ridiculously simplistic terms—for example, "experiencing a sense of moral obligation proves there is a God." Lewis did not say this and did not think this. As with the "argument from desire," his argument is, rather, that the common human experience of a sense of moral obligation is easily and naturally accommodated within a Christian framework.

For Lewis, experiences and intuitions—for example, concerning morality and desire—are meant to "arouse our suspicions" that there is indeed "Something which is directing the universe." We come to suspect that our moral experience suggests a "real law which we did not invent, and which we know we ought to obey,"[21] in much the same way as our experience of desire is "a kind of copy, or echo, or mirage" of another place, which is our true homeland. And as we track this suspicion, we begin to realize that it has considerable imaginative and explanatory potential. What was initially a dawning suspicion becomes solidified as a growing conviction that it makes sense of what matters to us naturally and persuasively.

So what can be learned from Lewis's approach? Perhaps I could mention two points in particular. First, Lewis helps us see that apologetics need not take the form of a slightly dull deductive argument, but can be understood and presented as an invitation to step into the Christian way of seeing things and explore how things look when seen from its standpoint. Try seeing things this way! If worldviews or metanarratives can be compared to lenses, which of them brings things into sharpest focus?

And second, we need to realize that Lewis's explicit appeal to reason involves an implicit appeal to the imagination. Perhaps this helps us understand why Lewis appeals to both modern and postmodern people. I see no historical evidence that compels me to argue that Lewis deliberately set out to do this, constructing a mediating position between two very different cultural moods. The evidence suggests that he saw things this way naturally and never formalized it in terms of a synthesis of these two very different modalities of thought. Rather, Lewis gives us a *synoptikon* that transcends the great divide between modernity and postmodernity, affirming the strengths of each and subtly accommodating their weaknesses.

Yes, Lewis affirms the rationality of the universe—but does so without plunging us into an imaginatively drab world of cold logic and dreary argumentation. Yes, Lewis affirms the power of images and narratives to captivate our imagination—but does so without giving up on the primacy of truth. As the churches face an increasingly complex cultural context in which they must preach and minister, Lewis offers insights and approaches that are potentially enriching—and, I venture to suggest, culturally plausible and intellectually persuasive.

In the end, Lewis tells the truth by showing the truth. He offers us an intellectually capacious and imaginatively compelling vision of the Christian faith, perhaps best summed up in his lapidary statement at the end of his essay "Is Theology Poetry?" Using a powerful visual image, Lewis invites us to see God as both the ground of the rationality of the world and the one who enables us to grasp that rationality. "I believe in Christianity as I believe that the Sun has risen, not only because I see it but because by it I see everything else."[22] This beautifully crafted sentence is a fitting memorial to both Lewis himself and his rich understanding of faith. How appropriate that it adorns the memorial to be unveiled in this Abbey tomorrow!

Let me end by noting an interesting parallel between Lewis and the great Genevan reformer John Calvin. Neither Lewis nor Calvin had any children, though both were stepfathers to children from their wives' earlier marriages. When Calvin was mocked by his critics for being childless, he offered an intriguing rebuttal. Anyone, he declared, who read his books and came to share his way of thinking was his child. And when seen that way, Calvin turned out to have rather a large family! I think the same is true of Lewis. Many of us find that our ways of thinking have come to be deeply shaped by Lewis; to put it another way, we share something of his intellectual DNA. None of his many admirers is a physical descendant of Lewis; yet we are all linked to him through our imagination and reason. Perhaps there will be even more to celebrate in another fifty years' time!

8

Listening and Engaging

John Stott on the Gospel and Our Culture

I n this chapter I want to explore one of the most interesting aspects of the theology of John Stott, which has particular relevance to bringing the Christian faith and our secular culture into conversation—namely, the notion of "double listening." This aspect of the discipleship of the mind is particularly important to Christian apologetics, allowing bridges to be built from the gospel to a wider culture beyond the churches. Yet it also opens up some deep theological questions, each worth exploring in its own right.

Stott is regarded by many—including myself—as one of the greatest and wisest evangelical voices of the twentieth century.[1] In 2005, *Time* magazine named Stott as one of the one hundred most influential living people in the world. His passing in July 2011 has, I think, helped us to appreciate at least something of his full significance. Too many evangelicals since then have naively assumed that the mere replication of Stott's style of preaching or the repetition of his theological commitments ensures the same success that he once

---

Based on lectures given at Central Hall, Westminster, London, on April 26, 2013.

enjoyed. This, it has to be said, reflects a rather shallow theology, which is lamentably inattentive to the significance of Stott's personal disposition and his character as a statesman. Stott developed these qualities as part of his personal discipleship, and they were arguably fundamental to his influence. Others may have talked about the realities of the Christian faith; Stott went further and embodied them.

Stott was more than an evangelical statesman, however; he was also one of the most gifted evangelists of his generation, noted for his reflection on the core themes of the gospel and their implementation in the life and witness of the churches. Stott has been a major influence on my own thinking, especially on apologetics and how we might communicate the Christian faith today. One of his finest reflections on this point is to be found in his book *Christian Mission in the Modern World*, based on a set of lectures given in Oxford in 1975.[2] I first read this work when I was serving in parish ministry in Nottingham in the early 1980s.[3] I read it again in preparation for this chapter and was struck by how little his analysis had dated. Perhaps the examples Stott provides might now need updating; the basic ideas underlying them, however, remain important and helpful.

Stott's fundamental point is that we need to develop a capacity for "double listening" if we are to avoid "the opposite pitfalls of unfaithfulness and irrelevance, and be able to speak God's Word to God's world with effectiveness today."[4] Stott's concept of "double listening" invites comparison with the German philosopher Hans-Georg Gadamer's notion of the "two horizons."[5] It demands immersion in both the text of Scripture and the lived realities of the world around us, as a means of bringing the gospel into connection with the world, faithfully and effectively: "I believe we are called to the difficult and even painful task of 'double listening.' That is, we are to listen carefully (although of course with differing degrees of respect) both to the ancient Word and to the modern world, in order to relate the one to the other with a combination of fidelity and sensitivity."[6]

For Stott, there is only one gospel, and we are not at liberty to play around with this. Nevertheless, we must acknowledge what he terms a "solemn responsibility to reinterpret it in terms meaningful to our own culture."[7] And this involves an act of theological translation, in which the gospel is interpreted in terms that our culture can understand.

Yet before we engage with Stott's notion of "double listening" more fully, we need to explore some issues that hover in the background of his discussion of the effective yet faithful communication of the Christian gospel. One of the first questions we must address, Stott observes, is whether the New Testament presents us with only one formulation or articulation of the gospel. After assembling his evidence, Stott argues that we must affirm that there is "only one basic apostolic tradition of the gospel," while at the same time pointing out that "the apostolic approach was 'situational'"—in other words, that "different situations called forth different treatments."[8]

In my view, Stott is quite right on both points. The way the New Testament uses the term "gospel" clearly implies that it is something that is shared within and across the Christian communities of the early Christian world. Yet the New Testament also witnesses to a diversity of renderings of the gospel—something that is, I think, especially clear in the sermons recorded in the Acts of the Apostles, which is probably our most important witness to the early Christian preaching of the gospel, as opposed to Christian reflection on the intellectual and practical implications of the gospel, primarily found in the New Testament Letters.

Stott makes this point by inviting us to compare the very different approaches adopted by Paul in his sermon in the synagogue in Antioch and his address to the Areopagus in Athens; I would suggest that this point is made clearer still by comparing both of these with Peter's great sermon on the day of Pentecost. It is the same gospel that is being proclaimed in each situation, to be sure—but we must note and respect the very different articulations of that gospel, reflecting the different audiences and their situations.

In his Pentecost sermon (Acts 2), addressing a Jewish audience, Peter quotes extensively from the Old Testament and shows how Jesus Christ fulfills its hopes. In his Areopagus speech (Acts 17), addressing a secular Greek audience who knew nothing about the Old Testament, Paul draws on ideas from Greek culture and poetry to convey some central gospel themes. It is indeed the same gospel; yet the mode of articulation is quite distinct, reflecting the different cultural contexts being engaged.[9]

Stott thus considers whether the gospel is to be thought of as "culturally conditioned" on account of the historical and cultural circumstances of its original formulations and whether this requires that we make appropriate cultural adaptations in our own preaching of the gospel today. Stott begins by noting that God's revelation took place in a specific cultural context and, in order to grasp it properly, we need to be able to "think ourselves back into that culture."[10] I think this is very clear. We must be careful to read the New Testament in its own context.

Stott's point is that the New Testament is indeed a revealed document, but it is one that was revealed in a specific historical and cultural location and uses aspects of that cultural context to communicate God's truth—such as cultural norms and vocabulary. To give an obvious example: we cannot appreciate the full significance of the father's actions on seeing his son returning in the parable of the prodigal son (Luke 15:11–32) unless we are aware that, in terms of the culture of the day, running to meet someone was seen as undignified. That's why an ahistorical reading of the New Testament is as impossible as it is meaningless.

Stott immediately and rightly also makes a counterpoint. This does not mean that the gospel is limited to its original historical and cultural context or that we are forced to cut our thinking loose from Scripture in order to connect up with contemporary culture:

"It is comparatively easy to be faithful if we do not care about being contemporary, and easy also to be contemporary if we do not bother to be faithful."[11]

Now I cannot help but think that, while Stott articulates a useful principle, the difficulties really begin to emerge as we try to apply it. I will gladly defend him here, however. Stott helps clarify the parameters of our reflection, identifying the tasks we must undertake. We cannot simply read out the words of the New Testament and expect our readers to understand them; we need to interpret them and translate them into the cultural vernacular. Yet this process of interpretation and translation takes place within a certain framework, which both informs and limits what we can do.

Let us also remember that every act of translation from the Greek of the New Testament into English is an act of interpretation! In trying to translate Paul's important term *dikaiōsis* into English, we end up having to interpret it, whether immediately or subsequently.[12] If we translate it as "justification," we still have to explain what this word means, as most would now understand the normal English sense of that word to mean offering an explanation for our actions or getting the right-hand margins of a document aligned on our computers. If we paraphrase the word, we have to defend the alternative forms of words that we use. You might think of Eugene Peterson's paraphrase of Romans 5:1 in *The Message*, where he interprets justification as to "set us right with [God], make us fit for him" or the Good News translation—now showing its age—that renders the opening part of the verse as, "Now that we have been put right with God through faith."

There is indeed a tension between being faithful and contemporary—that is to say, faithful to Scripture and contemporary in our communication.[13] Stott is clearly implying that this is a *creative* tension, however, that opens up space for us to maintain theological integrity on the one hand and cultural relevance on the other. This, of course, is the basic principle Stott expressed in his notion of "double listening," which probably received its definitive formulation in his landmark book *The Contemporary Christian* (1992), the British edition of which was famously subtitled "An Urgent Plea for Double Listening." (For reasons that I don't quite understand, the American edition altered this to "Applying God's Word to Today's World"—a nice turn of phrase, yet it doesn't make quite the same point.)

Stott understood "double listening" as embodying an attentiveness toward Scripture on the one hand and the cultural idioms and rational habits of the secular world on the other. His objective was to allow the richness of the Christian gospel to be communicated to the world, in terms that it could understand: "We listen to the Word with humble reverence, anxious to understand it, and resolved to believe and obey what we come to understand. We listen to the world with critical alertness, anxious to understand it too, and resolved not necessarily to believe and obey it, but to sympathize with it and to seek grace to discover how the gospel relates to it."[14] It is not enough to understand the world of the New Testament; we are called on to connect the gospel with a world outside the church and thus unfamiliar to many who are engaged in professional Christian ministry. This calls for an act of cultural and intellectual empathy, in which the preacher tries to inhabit two worlds and forge bridges between them.

Stott found a precedent for this approach in the writings of Arthur Michael Ramsey (1904–88), archbishop of Canterbury from 1961 to 1974. Ramsey suggested that the Christian churches needed to enter into the minds and souls of whose who had no connection with the church or who had lost whatever connections they once had: "We state and commend the faith only in so far as we go out and put ourselves inside the doubts of the doubters, the questions of the questioners and the loneliness of those who have lost their way."[15] Although critical of Ramsey at other points, Stott clearly felt that such an act of empathy was both necessary and possible: "Unless we listen attentively to the voices of secular society, struggle to understand them, and feel with people in their frustration, anger, bewilderment and despair, weeping with those who weep, we will lack authenticity as the disciples of Jesus of Nazareth. Instead, we will run the risk (as has often been said) of answering questions no one is asking, scratching where nobody is itching, supplying goods for which there is no demand."[16]

Christian preachers needed to listen to the world in order to understand its cries of pain and the sighs of the oppressed. Yet this listening demanded skills of those who felt called upon to undertake it, above all a deep immersion in the world of Scripture and secular Western culture.

So how do we "listen to the world"? Stott himself set out two main approaches, both of which were incorporated into his own ministry: first, through private conversations with experts in various fields, which lie behind Stott's sermons on issues facing Christians today—such as industrial relations and economic issues; second, through reading groups, such as that which Stott began in 1958 at All Souls, Langham Place, and which he developed further during the 1970s.[17] The "reading group" initially consisted of about a dozen young graduates and professional people, "all of whom were modern young men and women anxious to relate the gospel to the modern world."[18] The books that they read included Richard Dawkins's *Selfish Gene* (1976). But how well, we must ask, did they understand it? Reading groups are prone to misread the texts under consideration, especially when these lie outside the group's cultural and academic competencies. Recent historical study has suggested that the culture represented at All Souls, Langham Place during the late 1960s and early 1970s was sociologically limited.[19] All Souls remained a stubbornly middle-class enclave, and this inevitably affected Stott's cultural judgments on the one hand and his theological translations into the cultural vernacular on the other.

If Stott's concept of "double listening" is to be criticized, it is in the manner it was implemented, which in effect (though not in intention) made it dependent on "filters" of the reading groups at All Souls.

The aim of listening more attentively and intelligibly to the modern world cannot be faulted. Yet while the questions raised by members of Stott's reading group might illuminate how these Christians understood secular culture, in particular why they found it so problematic, this does not cast much light on how secular culture (mis)understands Christianity. It has always seemed to me that the best way for Christians to enter into a secular mind-set is not through reading books, but through encouraging Christians to be citizens of both worlds and thus helping their fellow Christians to bridge the gap between the church and the world. Someone who is bilingual does not need a translator.

Stott himself clearly grasped the nettle of translating theology into the cultural vernacular. In my view, one of his best attempts to do this is to be found in his 1982 book *Between Two Worlds*, in which he explores the role of the preacher as the one who bridges the world of Scripture and the contemporary world, allowing the realities of the gospel to be grasped by the audience. It is an outstanding work of its kind, showing how the significance of Jesus Christ can be "translated" into the idioms of modern culture. A short extract will help illustrate this point: "To encounter Christ is to touch reality and experience transcendence. He gives us a sense of self-worth or personal significance, because He assures us of God's love for us. He sets us free from guilt because He died for us and from paralyzing fear because He reigns."[20] All of these statements are thoroughly grounded in the New Testament. Yet Stott has succeeded in "translating" them, not simply in the sense of making them intelligible but in the deeper sense of enabling the gospel to connect with contemporary cultural concerns, moods, and anxieties. In doing this, Stott does not seek to deny or downplay the role of the Holy Spirit in biblical interpretation but simply to carry out the responsibility of the office of the preacher.

So what is this gospel? Stott's answer is brilliant and arresting in its simplicity: "God's good news is Jesus."[21] As the study of Christian history makes clear, each generation has tried to translate the foundational idea that "God's good news is Jesus" into its own cultural vernacular, while remaining faithful to Scripture. I fully concede that some of those attempts were misguided, some were well-intentioned yet flawed, and others were simply brilliant. Yet all are provisional statements of the gospel within a cultural context; none is final, precisely because culture changes and we cannot leave the gospel stranded by insisting that it be stated in some specific historical form, well adapted to the past but useless on today's streets.

Christianity needs to be explained. The Bible needs to be interpreted and applied. And both involve us, as active agents, doing our best to translate the realities of the gospel into the categories of the contemporary—not to reduce the gospel to contemporary ideas but to allow it to gain access to people's minds and lives, so that it can begin its work of transformation and renewal. Stott was a master of the art of cultural translation, seeing this as opening doors for the entry of the gospel into the souls of his audiences.

Let me return to Stott's landmark statement: "God's good news is Jesus." When I first read those words, I was thrilled. I was getting fed up with dry and overintellectualized theories about Jesus Christ that were often presented as if the theories were somehow to be equated with the gospel or represented the totality of the New Testament witness to its central figure. Stott's reflections on some passages describing early Christian evangelism in Acts led him to this powerful conclusion, which I hope is uncontroversial: "Jesus Christ is the heart and soul of the gospel."[22] I found this recall to basics to be both refreshing and liberating. And, in my view, Stott's wisdom at this point must be given due weight in our thinking.

The gospel is about what J. Oswald Sanders (1902–92) called "Christ incomparable"—to borrow the title of his classic devotional work of 1952.[23] As one of the greatest missionary strategists of his day, Sanders knew that Jesus Christ had to be proclaimed in all his radiance, wonder, and glory. There was no place for proclaiming a reduced and impoverished Christ to the world. To challenge and persuade the world, we must proclaim Christ to the world in all his fullness and wonder. Furthermore, Sanders alerts us to the dangers of focusing simply on expository correctness, which can too easily lead to a focus on the biblical text that unhelpfully diverts attention from its substance—the living reality of Jesus Christ.

It's a point that is made frequently in the writings of C. S. Lewis, who often points out that we risk substituting a theory about Jesus for the living personal reality of Jesus. The gospel is not a theory; it is a person. Now of course we need to explain why this person is so significant, and that involves interpretation. Yet this interpretation is to be *added* to the personal reality of Christ; what concerns me is that some are *reducing* the personal reality of Christ to the affirmation of right verbal formulas about him. This represents, as J. I. Packer shrewdly observed, a doctrine of "justification by words"—signaling theological orthodoxy at a purely verbal level.

I see this problem as lying behind one of the more worrying features of British evangelicalism today—a failure to produce devotional works of the caliber of those which so enriched the spiritual lives of earlier generations and helped them in their quest for spiritual growth. I have already mentioned Sanders's *Christ Incomparable*; we might easily add other classics, such as Oswald Chambers's *My Utmost for His Highest*, published in 1924. A fetish for excessive theological precision and an impoverishing move toward seeing Christ through reductive theoretical frameworks has led to a loss of devotional focus here—not least because it encourages an unhelpful tendency to think of "growth in faith" in terms of familiarization with theological theories rather than with a deepened love for, and commitment to, Jesus Christ. Discipleship is about following Christ, not simply locating him at the right place on a theological map.

Let me make it clear that I write these words as someone who repeatedly insists on the importance of theology and affirms the critical importance of grasping the true identity and significance of Christ, which is safeguarded by the theological framework of the creeds, especially the Nicene Creed.[24] My concern is those who detach doctrines about Christ from the person of Christ, as he is known and encountered through prayer and worship. Rightly understood, such doctrines are walls and fences, designed to preserve what is essential and special about Jesus Christ. Yet the church is called to proclaim Christ, not preach about walls and fences.

It is time to draw the threads of this chapter together. I have often been struck by some words of the Swiss theologian Emil Brunner, in his important reflections on Christian mission. For Brunner, the gospel demanded and deserved constant rearticulation and restatement, without losing sight of its changeless and timeless relevance: "There is indeed an *evangelium perennis* but not a *theologia perennis*. . . . The gospel remains the same, but our understanding of the gospel must ever be won anew."[25] We have work to do, in stating the gospel in terms and genres that can connect with our audiences, listening to them as we try to use their language to express the realities of the gospel. The challenge is to ensure that we navigate a proper trajectory between being faithful to Scripture and capable of connecting with contemporary culture. That, I suggest, is where the real debate lies—how best to do this. And I suggest further that it is part of the process of discipleship, as we try to value the legacy of our past without being locked into a dead and bygone world.

Stott thus sets out an aspect of the discipleship of the mind that seems to me to be of critical importance. As part of our growth in faith, we are called upon to know both the Christian faith and the wider culture that lies beyond the walls of the church, with a view to bringing these into conversation. My own work at the interface of Christianity and the natural sciences has made me aware of the importance of this theme and brought home to me how we need to encourage others to inhabit the borderlands of faith and culture. Stott's call for a "double listening" remains a wise strategy; we need even greater wisdom today in working out how to implement it in an increasingly complex and fragmented culture.

9

J. I. Packer on Theology and Spirituality

In this chapter, I would like to reflect on the significance of J. I. Packer—"Jim" to his friends—for Christian discipleship. Let me begin with an obvious question. Some twenty years ago, I wrote a theological biography of Packer.[1] So why did I do that? Indeed, why do I keep on writing theological biographies? After all, I recently wrote major intellectual biographies of C. S. Lewis (2013) and the neglected Swiss theologian Emil Brunner (2014).[2] Well, let me tell you why.

All too often, we think of theology simply in terms of abstract ideas and of theologians simply as repositories of those ideas—people who carry disembodied ideas around in their heads and are capable of dispensing them on demand. By writing a theological biography, I find I am able to explore how the core ideas of Christianity change people, by becoming part of their lives. In other words, it helps me appreciate and illuminate the capacity of Christianity to

A lecture given at the Evangelical Theological Society meeting in San Antonio, Texas, on November 17, 2016.

111

transform lives—including the way we think. In Romans 12, Paul therefore urges his readers not to be conformed to the world but to be transformed by the renewal of their minds.

As I talked to Packer back in the 1990s about his theological development and followed through the exposition and exploration of those ideas in his many writings, I came to realize how theology is about reflective inhabitation of the Christian faith. I see that understanding of theology in Packer himself and in the Puritan writers Packer rightly loves and admires so much. So the first point I want to make is simply this: Packer demonstrates how theology, when it is well done and when it is properly done, changes lives. It is not simply about the mere adjustment of our ideas; it is about the renewal of our minds and, subsequently, the redirection and reinvigoration of our lives.

Let me explore a few themes that illuminate Packer's importance for theology in general. One of Packer's most characteristic emphases is our need for theology to keep a check on the kind of loose thinking that arises from an uncritical personal piety. Now I think that such piety is on the whole a good thing. I adore Jesus Christ as my Lord and Savior and don't feel in the least embarrassed to speak in such explicitly relational terms about Christ. But there is a danger here—a danger to which Packer is acutely alert. Personal piety can easily degenerate into uncritical thinking about faith, leading us into all kinds of inadequate judgments. Packer brought this out clearly in one of his earliest published writings—a 1955 review, published in the *Evangelical Quarterly*, of a leading work promoting the Keswick holiness teaching of that period. Listen to this theological one-liner from that review: "Pelagianism is the natural heresy of zealous Christians who are not interested in theology."[3]

You can't help but admire the theological concision and insight of that sentence. As his colleagues at Regent College Vancouver often quip, "Packer by name, Packer by nature!" One of Packer's great strengths is his capacity to condense—to offer succinct summaries

of often complex and highly nuanced topics. He locates the fundamental problem as lying in a misdirected enthusiasm for personal
devotion, which is inattentive to the evangelical realities of human
nature on the one hand and to the transformative power of God's
grace on the other.

That's why it's important to think theologically. When I was writing my biography of Packer back in the 1990s, I got in touch with
many of his students from the late 1950s at Tyndale Hall, Bristol,
which was then a theological college of the Church of England.
They remembered Packer well. And one of the things they treasured
about him was his willingness to talk about theology over the college breakfast table. They would ask him about the great theological
questions of the day—the relationship between divine sovereignty
and human freedom, to give one obvious example. What they valued
was the style of Packer's replies. He did not give them prepackaged
answers; he showed his theological working. As one of them told
me, Packer taught them how to theologize—to develop their own
theological frameworks, not simply to parrot other people's answers.
They found him to be an invaluable theological resource. I want to
echo their judgment. In his lecture courses at Bristol in the 1970s
and at Regent College over the last few decades, Packer showed
his students how to do theology for themselves rather than simply
presenting them with the outcomes of that process.

One aspect of Packer's approach to theology that has always impressed me is his rigorous grounding of theological reflection in an
engagement with the Bible. If you search the archive of recordings
of presentations given at Regent College Vancouver, you will find a
rich treasure trove of Packer's lectures on the Bible. For example, he
offered two courses of lectures at the 2016 Regent College summer
school: one on the Anglican Heritage; the other on the Letter to the
Colossians. There is always a risk that systematic theology becomes
independent of the Bible. Evangelicals, of course, would say that we
never do this. In reality, however, I think sometimes we do, even if

unintentionally—for example, by adopting template approaches to theology, which means that we read Scripture in the light of preconceived theological schemes and do not allow these to be challenged or informed by the biblical text. Packer's principled attentiveness toward the biblical text is, to my mind, a clear theological virtue.

So how do we read the Bible? One of the many criticisms often directed against evangelicalism is that it represents a highly individualist reading of the Bible—what Packer himself styled a "Lone Ranger" approach, adopted by people who have "proudly or impatiently" turned their backs on the church and their heritage.[4] I do not for one moment dispute the importance of grounding biblical truth in the lives of individuals, but as we all know, there is a danger that individual perspectives and judgments become theologically determinative: this is how I see things—so this is how things really are.

What can we do about this? Packer offers us the beginnings of an answer, which I personally continue to find generative and helpful. We must learn to read the Bible in company. Here is how he described his own approach to theology back in 1996 in his masterly essay "On from Orr: The Cultural Crisis, Rational Realism, and Incarnational Ontology": "I theologize out of what I see as the authentic biblical and creedal mainstream of Christian identity, the confessional and liturgical 'great tradition' that the church on earth has characteristically maintained from the start."[5] For Packer, "keeping regular company with yesterday's great teachers" helps us to open our eyes to wisdom that might otherwise be denied to us.[6] And Packer has remained faithful to his own principles. Think of his detailed studies of the relevance of the Puritans for today's church. Packer's love for the Puritans was not born out of antiquarian curiosity but out of a burning conviction that there was gold in the Puritan hills. He had discovered this personally and wanted to share this wisdom with others.[7]

Packer found in Puritanism a movement that was theologically rigorous yet pastorally and spiritually engaged. In many of his writings of the 1990s, we find Packer turning to the treasure chest of Christian heritage and opening up its riches for contemporary Christianity. There was no artificial detachment imposed here between Christian theology and the Christian life. Like the Puritans, Packer is an ecclesially engaged theologian, who sees the natural place of the theologian as lying within the community of faith—not standing above the people of God, still less standing outside them, but, rather, speaking to them as one who shared their journey of faith and hoped to encourage them to reflect on it more rigorously and profoundly.

There is an important point here that we need to grasp and appreciate. We find it also in the writings of C. S. Lewis. Both Packer and Lewis deplore "chronological snobbery"—the idea that somehow the most recent is the best; that the past is somehow discredited or rendered useless by the passage of time. Both invite us to reach into the past and retrieve its riches—not uncritically, for they made mistakes in the past, just as we do today. Yet the passage of time has helped us to see how some theologies retain their power and perceptiveness, inviting us to retrieve them and put them to fresh use today.

This has important implications for how we study historical theology. In studying the past, we can think of ourselves as stepping into the laboratory of faith, seeing how ideas were developed and explored and checked out against their biblical moorings, their apologetic potential, and their capacity to deepen our love for God—to mention just three criteria, to which many more could be added.

Packer gives evangelical Christians a conceptual framework that allows them to see writers like Luther, Calvin, and Jonathan Edwards (and many others) as helpful in informing and nourishing our faith, yet without displacing or undermining the Bible itself. To use Packer's own terminology, writers like Edwards play a ministerial, not a magisterial, role in our theologizing. For Packer, Edwards's reading of the Bible, and the way in which he applied it, can help us today—yet without disconnecting or distancing us from Scripture itself. The Christian past is like a quarry; we are invited to explore,

115

appropriate, and apply its riches—critically, of course, but also positively. We can even learn from past mistakes—which are sometimes made for the best of reasons.

The rich theological heritage of the past can help us enrich our vision of the Christian truth by allowing us to see the gospel with new eyes, refreshing our vision and challenging our limitations. I'm sure Packer would agree with C. S. Lewis, who, recognizing that his own eyes were not sufficient, declared that he would "see through those of others." Both Packer and Lewis develop their styles in dialogue with the classics of the past. Literature, for Lewis, enables us "to see with other eyes, to imagine with other imaginations, to feel with other hearts, as well as our own."[8] And that's what happens to me when I read Augustine, Luther, Calvin, Edwards—and Packer.

Now there's another point to emphasize here—Packer's insistence that theology and spirituality are inseparable. Yes, we all know that they are treated as different subjects in many seminaries. Yet I want to suggest that the distinction between them these days really reflects the etiquette of professional boundaries and the politics of professional guilds. Packer has long recognized the interconnection of theology and spirituality and saw this intimate connection embodied in Puritanism. He developed his interest in Puritanism shortly after his conversion, when he found some of its writings speaking deeply and persuasively to his own spiritual struggles.

Packer has quarried the Puritan tradition, helping his readers to see how a good grasp of Christian theology leads naturally and seamlessly into an authentic spirituality. The link between theology, prayer, and adoration has to be maintained and affirmed. While I see this emphasis throughout Packer's writings, I think it is fair to single out one work in particular as an exemplary statement of this general principle—his inaugural lecture of December 1989 as the first Sangwoo Youtong Chee Professor of Theology at Regent College, with the brilliant title "An Introduction to Systematic Spirituality." In that lecture, Packer stressed the utter impossibility of separating theology and spirituality. How, he asked, could anyone separate theology from the "relational activity of trusting, loving, worshipping, obeying, serving and glorifying God?"[9] Perhaps we can see a more extended application or exemplification of this approach throughout Packer's best-known work, *Knowing God*—but I think we find it in a more concentrated and explicit form in this inaugural lecture.

So, having just mentioned *Knowing God*, let me speak more fully about this rich and influential work, published in 1973. It has become a classic, and rightly so. There are so many things that can be said about this work, but I shall limit myself to two points. The first is the work's constant correlation of systematic theology and spirituality, which for Packer are really two sides of the same coin. This interweaving of understanding ideas and being transformed by them is integral to Christian discipleship. If I could put it like this, to grasp the Christian vision of God is also to be grasped by this vision of God—and transformed in terms of how we think and behave.

But there's a second point. The great theologian Athanasius of Alexandria, in his letters to Serapion in the fourth century, emphasized that words really matter in theology. Athanasius's concern was to find a terminology that is adequate to the great truths that stand at the core of the Christian faith, while stressing that we occasionally have to use nonbiblical terms to express biblical truths. I see this point echoed in *Knowing God*—the precise, weighed, and deliberate quest for the best words to express divine truth. Maybe Packer is like Flaubert, always questing for the elusive yet satisfying *mot juste*.

I would like to highlight one feature of *Knowing God* that strikes me as uncharacteristic of many theological works these days—namely, its elegant and clear prose. Packer avoids the dull technocratic writing style favored by some theologians and the pompous verbosity unfortunately cultivated by some others. Let me quote a few sentences from *Knowing God* to try to make my point.

What matters supremely, therefore, is not, in the last analysis, the fact that I know God, but the larger fact which underlies it—the fact that *he knows me*. I am graven on the palms of his hands. I am never out of his mind. All my knowledge of him depends on his sustained initiative in knowing me. I know him, because he first knew me, and continues to know me. He knows me as a friend, one who loves me; and there is no moment when his eye is off me, or his attention distracted from me, and no moment, therefore, when his care falters.[10]

Packer here shows us that good theology can be readable. The rhythms and cadences of these sentences are those of a preacher—a theologian who knows that words matter and so they must be chosen with great care and attention. Packer will think that I am flattering him, but I see obvious parallels here with the writings of C. S. Lewis. As I read *Knowing God*, I see Packer reflecting not simply the theological convictions of his Puritan forebears but also their passion to communicate those to both the hearts and minds of their audiences. As I remarked earlier, theologians are not empty vessels containing theological ideas but are living souls who exhibit and embody those ideas and values in their lives.

Now it would be cheap and easy for me to score theological points by quoting from other theologians whose writings do not perhaps exhibit the same verbal elegance and graciousness. Indeed, I could do this very effectively by quoting a few passages from my own works, but I will resist this temptation! Those of us who see ourselves as theologians need to reflect long and hard about how we express those truths verbally in our books, lectures, and sermons. And, yes, I did say sermons. I do not see how anyone could study Christian theology without longing to preach about the unsearchable riches of Christ!

I have only just begun to scrape the surface of Packer's rich engagement with the traditions and tasks of Christian theology. I hope, however, that even this very limited and inadequate account of his approach to theology will help you to realize how much we have to learn from Packer and those to whom Packer would point in the past as theological exemplars. The greatest tribute I can pay to Packer is simply to say that he has influenced and helped me. And as I know from many conversations and an extensive correspondence, there are many others who would say the same.

Let me end with a few words from Packer himself. In May 2016, Packer was asked what he hoped to achieve through his teaching for that year's summer school at Regent College. Here is his answer to that question: "What I shall be saying to my class, in substance, is: Look! This is the biggest thing that ever was! And we Christians, most of us, still haven't appreciated its size. We've been Christians for years and years, and yet we haven't fully grasped it."[11] For Packer, theology is about unpacking this "biggest thing that ever was"—faithfully and reliably. That is the evangelical core of preaching, prayer, proclamation, and adoration. It also stands at the heart of the joyful and prayerful discipleship of the mind that we call "theologizing."

PART 3

Journeying in Hope

Four Sermons

10

Truth, Mystery, and Darkness

On the Limits of Human Understanding

My theme in this sermon is "truth." In January 1697, the great English philosopher John Locke wrote to one of his closest friends explaining the delight he experienced in the pursuit of truth: "I know there is truth opposite to falsehood, that it may be found if people will, and is worth the seeking, and is not only the most valuable, but the pleasantest thing in the world."[1] Those words seem to me to be both an inspiration and a challenge. They could easily serve as the motto for the intellectual aspirations of the natural sciences, philosophy, and Christian theology.

However, Locke was also acutely aware of the limited capacity of reason to penetrate and comprehend the dark and strange world in which we live. In his *Essay concerning Human Understanding*, after surveying the significant problems we confront in trying to make sense of this world, Locke remarked, "From all which it is easy to

---

A university sermon preached before the University of Oxford at the University Church of St. Mary the Virgin, Oxford, on November 6, 2016.

perceive what a darkness we are involved in, how little it is of Being, and the things that are, that we are capable to know."[2] Locke's concern about the restricted scope of human reason was shared by many of his contemporaries. Think, for example, of Alexander Pope's *Essay on Man* (1732–34), which situates human life and reflection within a larger cosmic order. Yet we inhabit an unsettling, shadowy world that is not always transparent to us and the rationality of which is not always easy to perceive.

We are, Pope tells us, "born but to die, and reas'ning but to err."[3] We seem to be suspended somewhere in an indeterminate region between skepticism and certainty. Pope's famous declaration that humanity should study itself, not God, is often understood to arise from hostility toward religion or to reflect skepticism about theology as a discipline. Yet this amounts to a retrojection of present concerns onto the past. Pope's point is very different. He wants us to grasp that the limits placed on the human capacity to understand *anything*—let alone something so perplexing as the mystery of God—force us to focus on studying ourselves instead.

> Know then thyself, presume not God to scan,
> The proper study of mankind is man.[4]

Pope's *Essay on Man* invites us to reflect critically on the aspirations and limits of being human—to acknowledge the difficulties we face in trying to make sense of our universe, precisely because of the limits placed on the human capacity to reason. Pope concedes that this universe appears to be incoherent and ambiguous. Yet he insists that we have to acknowledge the frailty and fallibility of human moral and intellectual capacities in reaching this judgment. Maybe the universe does indeed appear to be imperfect and incoherent—yet perhaps this reflects the limits placed on human perception rather than the way things actually are. The poet John Keats later reworked Pope's approach in developing his concept of "negative capability"—

a willingness to embrace uncertainty, live with mystery, and come to terms with the inevitability of ambiguity.

Life seems chaotic and purposeless to us, precisely because we are immersed within the flux of things and cannot extricate ourselves from it to catch a full glimpse of reality. To use the famous image developed by the American theologian John Alexander Mackay, we long to stand on a balcony looking down on the road of life, which alone might be able to disclose that we have a meaningful place in a coherent universe. Yet our place is on the road, not the balcony. There is no privileged standpoint from which we can observe our world. We cannot stand above the flow of life and history, so we have to make sense of it from within.

The Irish writer John Banville, who won the Man Booker Prize in 2005 for his novel *The Sea*, is unquestionably worth listening to at this point. His earlier writings explore how many in the early modern period hope to find a certainty of meaning and truth in the natural sciences, seeing these as offering the most reliable source of human knowledge about the world in which we find ourselves. Banville points out how scientists such as Copernicus, Kepler, and Newton tried to discern the hidden order of our universe and live in accordance with it.

Now I think we can understand at least something of what they hoped to achieve. The philosopher Ludwig Wittgenstein suggested that we discover meaning and happiness when we believe that we are thinking and living in accordance with something deeper and greater than ourselves. We need to grasp that "big picture" of the universe and position ourselves within it—and that was what these scientific pioneers tried to do.

Yet, as Banville says, their quest for certainty proved elusive: "I saw a certain kind of pathetic beauty in the obsessive search for a way to be in the world, in the existentialist search for something that would be authentic."[5] This quest for authenticity was genuine, even passionate—but the intractability of the universe itself proved a frustration to the aspirations of these visionaries.

Gradually, the power of that vision faded, as it was forced to deal with the irreducible fragility and provisionality of human knowledge. Banville points out how the Western cultural investment in the natural sciences as tools of discernment of meaning proved to be misplaced. As its failure became more widely appreciated, Western culture experienced an unsettling transition from Cartesian certainty to Wittgensteinian despair. The hope of finding the Enlightenment's holy grail, the crystalline clarity of rationalist certainties, gradually gave way to a reluctant realization of the irreducible complexity of the world, which simply could not be expressed in terms of the clear and necessary ideas that the Enlightenment expected and demanded.

Banville chronicles the slow and irreversible transition from rational certainty to existential despair with graceful prose, which perhaps makes it easier for his readers to bear the troubling intellectual significance of what his words convey. For Banville, what one generation took to be rational certainties were found by a later generation to be simply cultural constructions. It's a problem that some, hankering after the certainties of the bygone Enlightenment, try to suppress, hoping that the rhetoric of what C. S. Lewis called a "glib and shallow rationalism" might distract people from noticing its striking lack of traction on reality.

While those rational certainties nowadays only seem to live on in the curious cultural backwater of the New Atheism, everyone else is trying to figure out how to cope with the predicament in which we find ourselves. Not even the natural sciences, it seems, can deliver secure answers to the deepest questions we would rightly ask ourselves about our meaning, value, and purpose. Yet this does not reduce us to despair; it simply highlights the importance of faith in making judgments that cannot be proved to be true, yet rightly command our intellectual loyalty as trustworthy.

For writers such as Dorothy L. Sayers and C. S. Lewis, Christianity offers a rational view of reality, which invites us to see ourselves and our strange world as they really are, not in terms that we

126

have constructed. For Sayers, Christianity was a discovery of a "big picture"—the way things actually are, not an artificial fabrication of our creative imaginations. Yet if there is indeed such a "big picture," we seem unable to grasp it fully by ourselves. We need help if we are to see things properly.

This, of course, is a classic theme of Christian theology. The notion of divine revelation is about the disclosure of a view of reality that we did not invent and that tantalizingly lies beyond the capacity of human reason to grasp fully. Revelation is not about the violation or usurpation of human reason but, rather, is a demonstration of its limits and disclosure or intimation of what is believed to lie beyond those limits. Revelation is about the illumination of the landscape of our world, so we can see things more clearly and grasp something of what lies beyond the scope of our vision, if only in part. As the apostle Paul put it, we "see through a glass, darkly" (1 Cor. 13:12 KJV), securing at best a partial glimpse of what we know to be a grander landscape.

For Christians, this capacity to see things as they really are—rather than as they are glimpsed from the surface of our world—is a gracious gift of God. Our eyes need to be opened, so that our perception of incoherence within the world is seen to arise from our inability to see fully and properly. Truth is about more than logical syllogisms; it is about the meaningful inhabitation of our world. Religious faith is thus not a rebellion against reason but, rather, a principled revolt against the imprisonment of humanity within the cold and limiting walls of a rationalist dogmatism. Human logic may be rationally adequate, but it is also existentially deficient.

Sadly, some of those who boast of being "freethinkers" are simply imprisoned by a defunct eighteenth-century rationalism, perhaps oblivious to the radical changes in our understanding of human rationality that have been forced on us in the last generation. The Enlightenment's appeal to the authority of reason as the ultimate arbiter of reality ends up being trapped in circular forms of argument.

Some assert that reason itself can demonstrate its own authority. To its critics, however, this is simply a circular and parasitical argument that both assumes and depends on its own conclusions. Reason judges reason. Yet if there were a flaw in human rational processes, reason itself would not be able to disclose this. We might find ourselves locked into unreliable patterns of thought, without any means of escape.

The recent rise of postmodernity is not really a symptom of cultural irrationalism, as critics such as Christopher Hitchens and Richard Dawkins suggest. Rather, it is a principled protest against the intellectual authoritarianism of rationalism and the inadequacy of its foundations. Perhaps we have only recently come to realize the deficiencies of an approach to life that is determined—as opposed to merely being informed—by reason. Reason is a wonderful critical tool; but it is an unreliable foundation for truth. It is too shallow to meet our existential needs on the one hand or to cope with the complexity of our universe on the other.

That's why the idea of "mystery" is so important, both scientifically and theologically. The great physicist Werner Heisenberg argued that scientific thinking "always hovers over a bottomless depth."[6] We are confronted with the "impenetrable darkness" of the universe and forced to face up to our acute difficulties as we struggle to find a language that is adequate to engage and represent this opaque world. Those of us who have studied quantum theory know how it was forced to develop its own distinct rationality to cope with our fuzzy world, which calls into question inadequate commonsense conceptions of what is reasonable, shaped by our limiting experience of reality. Human rationality must adapt to the structures of the universe rather than prejudge what they ought to look like on the basis of some naive predetermined notion of what is reasonable.

Similarly, Christian theology recognizes that it is utterly impossible to represent or describe God adequately using human language. Christian theology uses the term "mystery" to refer to the vastness of God, in that human images and words falter—if they do not break down completely—as they try to depict God fully and faithfully. A mystery is not something that is contradicted by reason but something that exceeds reason's capacity to discern and describe. To speak of some aspect of the natural world or of God as a mystery is not to try to shut down the human reflective process, but to stimulate it—by opening the mind to an intellectual vision that is simply too deep and broad to be fully apprehended by our limited human capacity to see, and challenging us to do our best to represent it within these limits.

Our universe is a mystery—something with so many impenetrable and uncomprehended dimensions that our minds struggle to take it in. We can only cope with such a mystery either by filtering out what little we can grasp and hoping that the rest is unimportant, or by slimming it down to what our limited minds can accommodate and, thus, simply reducing it to the rationally manageable. Yet both of these well-intentioned strategies end up distorting and disfiguring the greater reality we are trying to engage.

For many, the Christian doctrine of the Trinity represents a classic instance of the irrationality of faith. Augustine of Hippo offered us one of the finest accounts of the limits of our ability as human beings to capture God in slick little slogans. "If you think you have grasped God, it is not God who you have grasped."[7] *Si enim comprehendis non est Deus*: if you can get your mind around it, it's not God. It's something else that you might incorrectly think is God but, in fact, is something you have created and invented and labeled as God.

Anything that we can grasp fully and completely simply cannot be God, precisely because it would be so limited and impoverished. It is easy to create God in our own likeness—a self-serving human invention that may bear some passing similarity to God but actually falls far short of the glory and majesty of the God that stands at the heart of the Christian disclosure. In the end, our words are just not good enough to cope with the conceptual majesty of God, so splendidly expressed in the theological notion of glory. God simply overwhelms our mental capacities. The vastness of the reality that we inhabit simply cannot be grasped in anything other than a partial and limited manner by the human mind.

This university sermon today is set within the context of Christian worship. Perhaps the framework I have presented in this sermon may help us to understand the creative tension that exists within the Christian life between theology on the one hand and worship on the other. This tension reflects—and paradoxically celebrates—the fact that something of God can be grasped, however inadequately, by the human mind, hence leading to theology; at the same time it recognizes that so much of God still remains beyond the human capacity to understand, and hence leads to worship, in the sense of acknowledging that the greatness and majesty of God ultimately eludes verbal analysis and is therefore best expressed in the language and actions of praise and adoration.

The theme of darkness has hovered over this sermon, not because I am a creature of the night who relishes the shadowlands, but because we inhabit a world in which we can only see things in part. Locke and Heisenberg, in their different ways, call upon us to recognize the limits of our situation. Yet there is hope: the light shines in the darkness, which cannot overwhelm it. The rich vision of reality that stands at the heart of the Christian faith both captures our imagination and nourishes our mind. The Christian gospel allows us to make sense of our world and inhabit it meaningfully, while at the same time giving us a vision of hope for the greater reality that we believe awaits us in the New Jerusalem. It is, I trust, a fitting thought for us as we prepare to move into the season of Advent and focus on the Christian hope.

11

Intelligibility and Coherence

The Christian Vision of Reality

’ve always been struck by a phrase from the writings of Sir Peter
Medawar, a biologist who championed the public engagement of
science: "Only humans find their way by a light that illuminates
more than the patch of ground they stand on."[1] Human beings seem
to possess some desire to reach beyond the mechanics of engagement with our world, looking for deeper patterns of significance and
meaning. This does not mean, of course, that such patterns exist for
that reason! Yet there seems to be something about human identity
that involves a quest for something deeper. I hesitate to attempt a
distillation of the large body of research literature on this topic, but
it seems that we cope better with our complex and messy world if
we feel we can discern meaning and value within our own lives and
in the greater order of things around us.

Science is one of humanity's most significant and most deeply
satisfying achievements. In the sixth form at school, I focused on

---

The Hulsean Sermon, preached before the University of Cambridge at Great St.
Mary's Church, Cambridge, on March 1, 2015.

physics, chemistry, and mathematics. I gained a scholarship to Oxford University to study chemistry, and went on to do doctoral research at Oxford in the laboratories of Professor Sir George Radda, working on physical means of studying complex biological systems. Yet though I loved science as a young man, I had a sense that it wasn't complete. Science helped me to understand how things worked, but what did they mean? Science gave me a neat answer to the question of how I came to be in this world. Yet it seemed unable to answer a deeper question: Why was I here? What was the point of life?

The question is whether the natural sciences can help us engage with these deeper issues, which the philosopher Karl Popper famously termed "ultimate questions." For Popper, these were existentially significant questions, rooted in the depths of our being, yet that transcended the capacity of the natural sciences to answer. Popper isn't on his own here. The Spanish philosopher José Ortega (1883–1955), one of Spain's greatest philosophers, argued that we need more than the partial account of reality that science offers; we need a "big picture," an "integral idea of the universe" that possesses existential depth, not merely cognitive functionality.[2] Science has a wonderful capacity to explain, while nevertheless failing to satisfy the deeper longings and questions of humanity.

For Ortega, the great intellectual virtue of science is that it knows its limits, which are determined by its methods. It only answers questions that it knows it can answer on the basis of the evidence, but human curiosity wants to go further. We feel that we need answers to the deeper questions that we cannot avoid asking. Human beings want to press beyond the point at which science declares that it must stop. As Ortega rightly observed, human beings—whether scientists or not—cannot live without answering them, even in a provisional way: "We are given no escape from ultimate questions. In one way or another they are in us, whether we like it or not. Scientific truth is exact, but it is incomplete."[3]

There are two themes that stand out as important here—intelligibility and coherence. The first is easily grasped. We long for a framework that helps us make sense of what we observe around us and experience within us. I was drawn to Christianity partly because I sensed it allowed me to grasp and hold on to the intelligibility of our world, an insight expressed in C. S. Lewis's signature affirmation: "I believe in Christianity as I believe that the Sun has risen, not only because I see it, but because by it, I see everything else."[4] Yet there is another theme, hinted at so powerfully in our reading from the Letter to the Colossians (1:9–20)—the quest for coherence.

Christianity provides a web of meaning, a deep belief in the fundamental interconnectedness of things. It's like standing on top of a mountain and looking down at a patchwork of villages, fields, streams, and forests. We can take snapshots of everything we see. Yet what we really need is a panorama that holds the snapshots together, letting us see that there is a "big picture" and each of these little pictures has its place within the greater whole. The fear of many is that reality consists simply of isolated and disconnected episodes, incidents, and observations. Yet Christianity whispers reassurance here, providing us with a frame of vision that both illuminates our world and helps us to make it whole.

Our modern age has seen doubts about the coherence of reality, many arising from the "new philosophy" of the Scientific Revolution. Do new scientific ideas destroy any sense of a meaningful reality? The English poet John Donne (1572–1631) spoke movingly of this concern in the early seventeenth century, as scientific discoveries seemed to some to erode any sense of connectedness and continuity within the world. "'Tis all in pieces, all cohaerence gone," he wrote of this unsettling new world.[5] How could it be held together?

Christians find this theme eloquently engaged in the New Testament, as we saw from our reading, which speaks of all things holding together or being knit together in Christ (Col. 1:17). There is a hidden web of meaning and connectedness behind the ephemeral and incoherent world that we experience. This was the insight that constantly eluded the novelist Virginia Woolf (1882–1941), who occasionally experienced short, stabbing moments of clarity, which seemed to her to disclose "some real thing behind appearances."[6] These transitory and rare "moments of being" (as she called them) convinced her that there were hidden webs of meaning and connectedness behind the world she knew. Yet she could never enter this hidden world; it always seemed to retreat from her as she approached its door, as if she were grasping at smoke.

Christianity thus provides us with a reassurance of the coherence of reality—that however fragmented our world of experience may seem, there is a half-glimpsed "bigger picture" that holds things together, its threads connecting in a web of meaning what might otherwise seem incoherent and pointless. This theme resonates throughout the poetic and religious writings of the Middle Ages. As might be expected, it is a major issue in perhaps that greatest of medieval literary classics—Dante's *Divine Comedy*. As the poem draws to its close, Dante catches a glimpse of the unity of the cosmos, in which its aspects and levels are seen to converge into a single whole.[7]

So, have we lost sight of the idea of some deeper unity of reality? Where once there was a sense of intellectual and moral coherence to reality, there now seems to be what the German poet and novelist Hermann Hesse (1877–1962) once described as a mere aggregation of "intellectual fashions" and the "transitory values of the day."[8] Other intellectual developments have also posed a threat to the notion of a coherent reality, including Nancy Cartwright's idea of a "dappled world."[9] Where C. S. Lewis argued that "we are not reading rationality into an irrational universe, but responding to a rationality with which the universe has always been saturated,"[10] Cartwright holds that we are imposing an order or rationality when there may be none—or, indeed, there may be a variety of orderings, requiring multiple accounts of the natural world and its structures. For Lewis, we are responding to the universe as it actually is; for Cartwright, we run the risk of inventing our own universe and disregarding the one around us.

It seems to me that the Christian faith is able to enrich a scientific narrative by preventing it from collapsing into what John Keats described as a "dull catalogue of common things."[11] The sociologist Max Weber used the term "disenchantment" to refer to an excessively intellectual and rationalizing way of looking at nature that limited it to what could be measured and quantified. Now there will be scientists in this congregation, and they will perfectly reasonably point out that these processes are integral to the scientific method. And I agree. It's just that there's more that needs to be said. Science is really good at taking things apart so that we can see how they work. Faith is about putting them back together again so that we can see what they mean.

A religious perspective does not in any way deny the scientific utility of such a rationalizing approach. It simply insists that there is more that needs to be said if a full and satisfying account of reality is to be provided, and offers a supplementation of a scientific narrative by which this deeper and more satisfying account of life might be achieved.

The philosopher Mary Midgley is a leading defender of what she terms a "multiple maps" approach to grasping the depths and detail of reality. Midgley argues that we need "many maps, many windows" if we are to represent the complexity of reality, reflecting the fact that "there are many independent forms and sources of knowledge." She suggests that it is helpful to think of the world as a "huge aquarium": "We cannot see it as a whole from above, so we peer in at it through a number of small windows. . . . We can eventually make quite a lot of sense of this habitat if we patiently put together the data from different angles. But if we insist that our own window is the only one worth looking through, we shall not get very far."[12] For Midgley, no single way of thinking is adequate to explain, on its own, the meaning of our universe. "For most important questions in human life, a number of different conceptual tool-boxes always have to be used together."[13] If we limit ourselves to the methods of science in general, or one science (such as physics) in particular, we needlessly lock ourselves into a "bizarrely restrictive view of meaning."[14]

Midgley's basic principle of using multiple maps to represent a complex reality raises some challenges and some significant questions—such as the need to develop and deploy an appropriate interpretative framework to settle boundary disputes. Yet it also opens up some important possibilities for integration and enrichment of our vision. We need a rich palette of colors to represent the complexities of our observations of the world around us and our experiences within us.

My approach in this sermon is best described in terms of the "interweaving of narratives." Human beings construct their identities using multiple narratives. That's how we function as social animals. We weave together religious, political, social, and cultural narratives as we try to make sense of our world. It's natural for us to weave these threads together, just as it's natural for us to try to sort out how they interact—which takes priority—and how we resolve tensions or seeming contradictions between them. No one story, no one angle of gaze or tradition of investigation, is adequate to deal with human existence in all its richness and complexity.

This interweaving of narratives is essential as we try to deal with the "ultimate questions" that persistently refuse to go away. To answer these properly, we need to bring together multiple approaches and recognize the existence of multiple levels of meaning—such as purpose in life, values, a sense of individual efficacy, and a basis for self-worth.[15] What I am proposing is not some crude homogenization of narratives. They are like the patches of paint on an artist's palette; each color needs to be valued in its own right and used appropriately to render the rich texture and vibrancy of our world.

Perhaps I might offer an example to illustrate what I have in mind. I recall looking at the night sky in winter in the late 1960s and seeing the Belt of Orion—three bright stars in the constellation of Orion. I was an atheist back in those days, with no interest in God, but already knowing a deep sense of awe at the wonder of nature. I knew enough about astronomy to know that light took hundreds of years to travel to earth from those stars. To look at those stars was, in effect, to travel back in time. I was seeing them as they were, not as they are. I found the thought deeply troubling. Why? Because by the time the light now leaving those stars reached earth, I would be dead. Those stars became for me symbols of my own mortality, chilling silent reminders of the brevity of human life. The universe might be very beautiful, but it also seemed totally pointless.

It's a melancholy thought, known to many scientists who have written about their feelings of despair at the futility and utter pointlessness of the world that they are studying. Here's a good example. Ursula Goodenough, a biologist at the University of Washington, recalls being "overwhelmed with terror" at the thought of the immensity of the universe and the fact that it would one day come to an end. No longer could she appreciate the beauty of the stars; they came to represent or symbolize deeper and unsettling truths that she found unbearable. She wrote, "The night sky was ruined. I would never be able to look at it again. I wept into my pillow, the long slow tears of adolescent despair. . . . A bleak emptiness overtook me whenever I thought about what was really going on out in the cosmos or deep in the atom. So I did my best not to think about such things."[16] But what happens if you put on a different set of theoretical spectacles? What if the world is seen through a God lens? Through a Christian map of meaning? I discovered that the night sky looked rather different when seen from the standpoint of faith. Yes, it was still a symbol of immensity, against which I seemed insignificant. Yet I now realized that I mattered.

One of the world's most famous photographs was taken in 1990 from the Voyager space probe during its mission to study the outer solar system. Twelve years after its launch, it reached the planet Saturn and sent back images of that great planet. The astronomer

Carl Sagan suggested that the probe's cameras should be realigned to send back an image of earth, as seen from a distance of about six billion kilometers. After much discussion, NASA agreed. Back came the famous image of a "pale blue dot," set against the darkness of space—a "lonely speck in the great enveloping cosmic dark."[17] As Sagan rightly pointed out, this "distant image of our tiny world" set everything in perspective. How small, how insignificant, we are, compared with the vastness of space!

To this day, I keep on looking at that image from Voyager—that minuscule "pale blue dot" that is our cosmic home. I find my thoughts straying to one of the Psalms, which seems to anticipate the thoughts and emotions I now experience when looking at that "lonely speck in the great enveloping cosmic dark."

> When I look at your heavens, the work of your fingers,
> the moon and the stars that you have established;
> what are human beings that you are mindful of them,
> mortals that you care for them? (Ps. 8:3–4)

The psalm exults that human beings are part of God's creation and thus are named and loved by the God from whom all things come. Our lives are touched by transcendence, in that God chooses to relate to those whom he created.

We all need a greater narrative to make sense of the world and our lives, naturally weaving together multiple narratives and multiple maps to give us the greatest traction on reality. Reality is just too complex to be engaged and inhabited using only one tradition of investigation. We need the best picture of reality that we can devise if we are to inhabit it meaningfully and authentically. In my opinion, precisely such a view of reality is presented in the grand vision of the Christian faith. We are invited to inhabit and enact this vision, both in our lives and in the world, in the process of reflective habitation that stands at the heart of Christian discipleship.

12

Hope in the Darkness

t's always good to mark special occasions and think more deeply about the importance of these events. Merton College, Oxford, was founded 750 years ago. And while this is certainly something to celebrate, this occasion also invites us to reflect on deeper issues. In its long and distinguished history, this college has been through times of light and darkness. This year also marks the centenary of the outbreak of the First World War, an event that called into question the all-too-easy assumption that human beings are essentially rational and good. Those four years of brutal conflict were a dark time for this college, as they were for our nation. How, many asked, can we keep going in such dark times? What hope is there, that we can hold on to?

That need for hope remains important to all of us. We see it in our reading from the prophet Isaiah (Isa. 40:1–8). The people of Jerusalem were in exile in Babylon, far from their homeland. Would they ever return home? Those were dark times. And in the midst of

A sermon preached in Merton College Chapel on October 26, 2014, to mark the 750th anniversary of the college's foundation. I was a senior scholar at Merton College from 1976 to 1978.

that darkness, Isaiah spoke words of comfort and hope. God had not forgotten his people. They would return home! That hope sustained them as they waited for their liberation. Yes, they were still in exile. But they had hope for the future.

We need hope: not a naive and shallow optimism but a robust and secure confidence that there is something good—there is *Someone* good—who will triumph over despair and hopelessness. Many felt the need for that during the First World War—including a second lieutenant in the Lancashire Fusiliers who took part in the Battle of the Somme and went on to become a fellow of this college in 1945. His name was J. R. R. Tolkien. His epic work *The Lord of the Rings* was written and published during his time as Merton Professor of English, here at this college.

The Lord of the Rings is now widely regarded as one of the great works of English literature. One of its most distinctive themes is the reality of evil. Tolkien names evil, thus giving us permission to challenge the bland and inadequate moral outlook of our age that insists we respect everything. Like his close friend C. S. Lewis, Tolkien was convinced that we had lost the moral vocabulary that enabled us to speak of evil and, thus, to fight it.

But that is not the only theme we find so powerfully explored in Tolkien's epic work. It speaks of the role of the weak and powerless in changing the world for the better. That's why Hobbits—such as Frodo Baggins and his sidekick Sam—are so important. They are the little people, and in the end, they are the ones who make the difference. Tolkien also affirmed the reality of hope in the midst of despair and seeming helplessness. Listen to this passage, toward the end of *The Lord of the Rings*, when the victory of the forces of darkness seems assured: "There, peeping among the cloud-wrack above a dark tor high up in the mountains, Sam saw a white star twinkle for a while. The beauty of it smote his heart, as he looked up out of the forsaken land, and hope returned to him. For like a shaft, clear and cold, the thought pierced him that in the end the Shadow was

140

only a small and passing thing: there was light and high beauty for ever beyond its reach."[1]

That's the kind of hope that kept the people of Jerusalem going during their time of exile. Their God was beyond the reach of human tyranny and oppression, and one day things would change. That's the hope that keeps many of us going as well—the thought that there is something beyond this world of suffering and pain that we will one day enter and embrace. It's a theme we find so powerfully expressed in the New Testament's vision of the New Jerusalem, a world in which God has made everything anew and there is no more sorrow, pain, or death.

But there is another theme in *The Lord of the Rings* that speaks powerfully to us. As the work nears its end, the victory of evil seems inevitable. A dark mood settles over the narrative. And then everything changes. An unexpected event enables the ring to be destroyed, breaking the power of evil. Tolkien called this a *eucatastrophe*—a dramatic, unexpected event that disrupts a narrative of despair and redirects it toward the good.

For Tolkien, the best and greatest example of this radical upheaval of a story of hopelessness is the resurrection of Christ, a dramatic event that brought first astonishment, then hope—a real hope, grounded in something and Someone trustworthy. That is the hope that is to be seized and acted on, that keeps us going and keeps us growing, even in the darkest of times. The Christian hope of heaven raises our horizons and elevates our expectations—inviting us to behave on earth in the light of this greater reality. The true believer is not someone who disengages with this world in order to focus on heaven but someone who tries to make this world more like heaven.

Our readings today affirm the role of hope in a faithful God in sustaining us and inspiring us. "The grass withers, the flower fades; but the word of our God will stand forever" (Isa. 40:8). That hope in God, like Sam's vision of "light and high beauty," can never be taken away from us. It is right to celebrate that Merton College is 750 years

141

old—its vision of the transforming and enriching role of education as important today as it ever was—but the world around us has changed. Many of us feel that the optimism of an earlier generation has now receded. We are facing hard questions, difficult times, and uncertainties about the future, but we must not despair. "The word of our God will stand forever"—and we will stand with it.

13

The Hope of Heaven

The Christian faith is often compared to a journey through this world to the New Jerusalem. And as we travel, we often look backward to those who have made this journey before us, to those who have helped us in our journey of faith. C. S. Lewis worshiped here in this Oxford church from 1930 until his death fifty years ago this month. Though one of the most celebrated writers of his age, he was happy to be an ordinary member of this congregation. Some here will remember him personally, sitting in the same pew every Sunday with his brother, Warnie.

But others now will know him through his books and, curiously, that's probably how Lewis would want to be remembered. In the 1930s, Lewis declared that a writer is not a spectacle, who says, "Look at me!" Rather, a writer is more like a set of spectacles, who says, "Look through me!" Lewis gives us a way of looking at the world and ourselves that has proved deeply satisfying to both the mind and the soul. In one of his more memorable quotes, he declared that his faith in Christianity lay in its ability to illuminate reality. "I believe

A sermon preached at Holy Trinity Church, Headington Quarry, Oxford, on November 17, 2013, to mark the fiftieth anniversary of the death of C. S. Lewis.

in Christianity," he wrote, "as I believe that the Sun has risen—not only because I see it, but because by it I see everything else."[1]

The Christian faith, Lewis discovered, gave him a lens that brought things into focus. It was like turning a light on and seeing things properly for the first time. The powerful image of the sun rising and illuminating a dark landscape captures Lewis's basic conviction that Christianity makes sense of things—far more sense than the atheism he had embraced as a younger man. One of the themes that came to mean so much to him was the hope of heaven.

Like many other Christian writers before him, Lewis declares that the hope of heaven enables us to see this world in its true perspective. This life is the preparation for that greater reality. It is, as Lewis put it, the cover and title page of the "Great Story," in which every chapter is better than the one that went before.

For Lewis, this world is God's world and is to be valued, appreciated, enjoyed. Yet it is studded with clues that it is not our real home, that there is a still better world beyond its frontiers, and that one may dare to hope to enter and inhabit this better place. Lewis affirms the delight, joy, and purposefulness of this present life. Yet he asks us to realize that, when this finally comes to an end, something even better awaits us. Lewis believed that the secular world offers people only a hopeless end, and he wanted them to see and grasp the endless hope of the Christian faith and live in its light.

Does this mean that Lewis is a "world-denying" writer, who treats this world as devoid of value? No. Lewis was clear that to "aim at Heaven" is not to neglect this world or earthly concerns. Rather, it is to raise our horizon and elevate our expectations—and then to behave on earth in the light of this greater reality. We must try to infuse earth with the fragrance of heaven. The true believer is not someone who disengages with this world in order to focus on heaven but the one who tries to make this world more like heaven. Lewis was surely right when he declared that "the Christians who did most for the present world were just those who thought most of the next."[2]

As we look backward to remember Lewis, let us, like him, also look forward to anticipate heaven. As Lewis once remarked, "I must keep alive in myself the desire for my true country."[3] Some lines from chapter 15 of *The Last Battle*, the concluding novel of the Chronicles of Narnia, capture this point particularly well. On finally seeing the "new Narnia," Jewel the Unicorn declares, "I have come home at last! This is my real country! I belong here. This is the land I have been looking for all my life, though I never knew it till now."[4] For Lewis, the Christian hope is about returning home to where we really belong.

Lewis was no killjoy. He does not deny that we experience desire in this life, nor does he suggest that these desires are evil or a distraction from the real business of life. His point is that our desires cannot be, and were never meant to be, satisfied by earthly pleasures alone. They are "good images" or signposts of something "further up and further in."[5] They are foretastes of the true source of satisfaction that we will find in the presence of God. For Lewis, heaven is the "other country" for which we were created in the first place. We should, he declares, "make it the main object of life to press on to that other country and to help others do the same."[6]

This rich vision of heaven, deeply rooted in the New Testament, was something that brought Lewis hope, especially in the final years of his life. The Christian hope, Lewis insisted, was not, as he put it, some "form of escapism or wishful thinking" but was, rather, "a continual looking forward to the eternal world."[7] Hope is a settled state of mind in which we see this world in its true light and look forward to our final homecoming in heaven, trusting in Jesus Christ, who our gospel reading declared to be "the living bread that came down from heaven" (John 6:51). Lewis would surely have echoed the famous statement of Cyprian of Carthage, who was martyred for his faith in North Africa in the third century: "Paradise is our native land." Lewis shared Cyprian's hope at the thought of returning to his true homeland. And he would want us to share it as well.

Notes

Introduction

1. Edward O. Wilson, *Consilience: The Unity of Knowledge* (New York: Vintage, 1999), 294.

2. John Dewey, *The Quest for Certainty* (New York: Capricorn Books, 1960), 255.

3. Alister McGrath, *Mere Theology: Christian Faith and the Discipleship of the Mind* (London: SPCK, 2010).

4. For my own extended engagement with Lewis, see especially Alister E. McGrath, *C. S. Lewis—A Life: Eccentric Genius, Reluctant Prophet* (London: Hodder & Stoughton, 2013); *The Intellectual World of C. S. Lewis* (Oxford: Wiley-Blackwell, 2013).

5. C. S. Lewis, "Is Theology Poetry?," in *C. S. Lewis: Essay Collection and Other Short Pieces*, ed. Lesley Walmsley (London: Collins, 2000), 21.

6. José Ortega y Gasset, "Ideas y creencias," in *Obras Completas*, vol. 5, *1932–1940* (Madrid: Fundación José Ortega y Gasset, 2006), 661.

7. Ortega, "Ideas y creencias," 665. Ortega here clearly hints at Acts 17:28.

8. Ludwig Wittgenstein, *Culture and Value* (Oxford: Blackwell, 1994), 73.

9. See the two classic works of Dietrich Bonhoeffer, *Life Together* (London: SCM Press, 2015) and *The Cost of Discipleship* (London: SCM Press, 2015).

10. See Darren Webb, "Modes of Hoping," *History of the Human Sciences* 20, no. 3 (2007): 65–83; "Pedagogies of Hope," *Studies in Philosophy and Education* 32 (2013): 397–414.

11. John Macmurray, *Persons in Relation* (London: Faber and Faber, 1961), 171.

Chapter 1 The Lord Is My Light

1. For excellent explorations of this theme, see John R. W. Stott, *Your Mind Matters: The Place of the Mind in the Christian Life* (Leicester: InterVarsity, 1973);

James W. Sire, *Habits of the Mind: Intellectual Life as a Christian Calling* (Downers Grove, IL: InterVarsity, 2000).

2. The German term *Weltanschauung*, from which we get our English word "worldview," means "a perception of the world." For comment, see Paul G. Hiebert, *Transforming Worldviews: An Anthropological Understanding of How People Change* (Grand Rapids: Baker Academic, 2008).

3. See Hans Blumenberg, "Light as a Metaphor for Truth: At the Preliminary Stage of Philosophical Concept Formation," in *Modernity and the Hegemony of Vision*, ed. David Michael Levin (Berkeley: University of California Press, 1993), 30–62.

4. Harry Blamires, *The Christian Mind: How Should a Christian Think?* (London: SPCK, 1963).

5. See, for example, Alister McGrath and Joanna Collicutt McGrath, *The Dawkins Delusion? Atheist Fundamentalism and the Denial of the Divine* (London: SPCK, 2007).

6. Bertrand Russell, *A History of Western Philosophy*, 2nd ed. (London: George Allen & Unwin, 1961), xiv.

7. There are many points at which Russell explicitly identifies himself as an agnostic, in that he regarded the question of God to lie beyond proof: see especially Bertrand Russell, *Essays in Skepticism* (New York: Philosophical Library, 1963), 83–84; *Bertrand Russell Speaks His Mind* (London: Barker, 1960), 20. However, Russell was prepared to allow that he was an atheist in the uncritical popular sense of that term.

8. Austin Farrer, "The Christian Apologist," in *Light on C. S. Lewis*, ed. Jocelyn Gibb (London: Geoffrey Bles, 1965), 26.

9. For a penetrating critique of the evangelical failure to engage adequately with such intellectual and cultural questions, see Mark A. Noll, *The Scandal of the Evangelical Mind* (Grand Rapids: Eerdmans, 1994).

10. See especially Walter Schmithals, *The Theology of the First Christians* (Louisville: Westminster John Knox, 1997), 122–23, 146–51. See further Raymond Pickett, *The Cross in Corinth: The Social Significance of the Death of Jesus* (Sheffield: Sheffield Academic, 1997), 213–16; Edward Adams and David G. Horrell, eds, *Christianity at Corinth: The Quest for the Pauline Church* (Louisville: Westminster John Knox, 2004).

11. See Mark McIntosh, "Faith, Reason and the Mind of Christ," in *Reason and the Reasons of Faith*, ed. Paul J. Griffiths and Reinhart Hütter (New York: T&T Clark, 2005), 119–42.

12. This is a major theme in Lesslie Newbigin, *Foolishness to the Greeks: The Gospel and Western Culture* (Grand Rapids: Eerdmans, 1986).

13. C. S. Lewis, "Is Theology Poetry?," in *C. S. Lewis: Essay Collection and Other Short Pieces*, ed. Lesley Walmsley (London: Collins, 2000), 21.

14. Augustine of Hippo, *Confessions* 4.15.25. A useful account of this idea in English can be found in Mary T. Clark, *Augustine* (London: Continuum, 2005), 13–25.

15. For the development of this idea, see Steven Marrone, *The Light of Thy Countenance: Science and Knowledge of God in the Thirteenth Century* (Leiden: Brill, 2001).

16. Henry Miller, *On Writing* (New York: New Directions, 1964), 37.

17. This ode is found in the preface to Chaucer's *Legend of Good Women*; see *The Complete Works of Geoffrey Chaucer*, ed. Walter W. Skeat, vol. 3 (Oxford: Clarendon Press, 1900), 58–76.

18. Michael Lackey, "'God's Grandeur': Gerard Manley Hopkins' Reply to the Speculative Atheist," *Victorian Poetry* 39 (2001): 83–90.

19. A point emphasized by John Polkinghorne, *Science and Christian Belief* (London: SPCK, 1994).

20. Paul Davies, *The Mind of God: Science and the Search for Ultimate Meaning* (London: Penguin, 1992), 77.

21. Albert Einstein, "Physics and Reality" (1936), in *Ideas and Opinions* (New York: Bonanza, 1954), 292.

22. John Polkinghorne, *Science and Creation: The Search for Understanding* (London: SPCK, 1988), 20–21. More recently, see John C. Polkinghorne, "Physics and Metaphysics in a Trinitarian Perspective," *Theology and Science* 1 (2003): 33–49.

23. Robin Collins, "A Scientific Argument for the Existence of God: The Fine-Tuning Design Argument," in *Reason for the Hope Within*, ed. Michael J. Murray (Grand Rapids: Eerdmans, 1999), 47–75.

24. See, for example, Rodney D. Holder, *God, the Multiverse, and Everything: Modern Cosmology and the Argument from Design* (Aldershot: Ashgate, 2004).

25. Alister E. McGrath, *A Fine-Tuned Universe: The Quest for God in Science and Theology* (Louisville: Westminster John Knox, 2009).

26. Terry Eagleton, *Reason, Faith, and Revolution: Reflections on the God Debate* (New Haven: Yale University Press, 2009), 28.

27. Eagleton, *Reason, Faith, and Revolution*, 87–89.

28. See the critical analysis in Margaret Archer, Andrew Collier, and Douglas V. Porpora, *Transcendence: Critical Realism and God* (London: Routledge, 2004), 12–13.

Chapter 2 Belief

1. I have made use of the ideas set out in this chapter in several of my books, especially Alister McGrath, *Faith and the Creeds* (London: SPCK, 2013); Alister McGrath, *The Landscape of Faith: An Explorer's Guide to the Christian Creeds* (London: SPCK, 2018).

2. Letter to Edward Sackville-West, quoted in Michael De-la-Noy, *Eddy: The Life of Edward Sackville-West* (London: Bodley Head, 1988), 237.

3. Henry Miller, *Big Sur and the Oranges of Hieronymus Bosch* (New York: New Directions, 1957), 25.

4. John M. Russell, *From Nineveh to New York: The Strange Story of the Assyrian Reliefs in the Metropolitan Museum and the Hidden Masterpiece at Canford School* (New Haven: Yale University Press, 1997).

5. Ludwig Wittgenstein, *Culture and Value* (Oxford: Blackwell, 1994), 73.

6. Ludwig Wittgenstein, *Philosophical Investigations* (Oxford: Blackwell, 2001), §610.

7. John of Salisbury, *Metalogicon*, iii, 4.

8. *Catechetical Lectures* 5.12, quoted in "Cyril of Jerusalem on the Role of the Creeds," in *The Christian Theology Reader*, ed. Alister E. McGrath, 5th ed. (Malden, MA: Wiley Blackwell, 2017), 78.

9. "The Elixir," in *The Works of George Herbert*, ed. F. E. Hutchinson (Oxford: Oxford University Press, 1941), 184.

10. Thomas à Kempis, *The Imitation of Christ*, book 1, chapter 3; my translation.

Chapter 3 Habits of the Christian Mind

1. C. S. Lewis, *Mere Christianity* (London: HarperCollins, 2002), 165.

2. See the rich material assembled in Mark J. Boda and Gordon T. Smith, eds., *Repentance in Christian Theology* (Collegeville, MN: Liturgical Press, 2006).

3. For this analogy, see Alister McGrath, *The Landscape of Faith: An Explorer's Guide to the Christian Faith* (London: SPCK, 2018).

4. Mary Healy, "Knowledge of the Mystery: A Study of Pauline Epistemology," in *The Bible and Epistemology: Biblical Soundings on the Knowledge of God*, ed. Mary Healy and Robin Parry (Milton Keynes: Paternoster, 2007), 134–58.

5. Augustine of Hippo, *Sermon* 88.5.5.

6. Rowan Williams, "Teaching the Truth," in *Living Tradition: Affirming Catholicism in the Anglican Church*, ed. Jeffrey John (London: Darton, Longman & Todd, 1991), 41.

7. See Stanley Hauerwas, *Vision and Virtue: Essays in Christian Ethical Reflection* (Notre Dame, IN: University of Notre Dame Press, 1974).

8. Stanley Hauerwas, "The Demands of a Truthful Story: Ethics and the Pastoral Task," *Chicago Studies* 21, no. 1 (1982): 65–66.

9. See Jennifer A. Herdt, "Alasdair MacIntyre's 'Rationality of Traditions' and Tradition-Transcendental Standards of Justification," *Journal of Religion* 78, no. 4 (1998): 524–46; Jean Porter, "Tradition in the Recent Work of Alasdair MacIntyre," in *Alasdair MacIntyre*, ed. Mark C. Murphy (Cambridge: Cambridge University Press, 2003), 38–69.

10. Stanley Hauerwas, *The Peaceable Kingdom: A Primer in Christian Ethics* (Notre Dame, IN: University of Notre Dame Press, 1983), 101–2. The classic idea of the *polis* (city-state) offers an illuminating way of developing Hauerwas's approach: see Arne Rasmusson, *The Church as Polis: From Political Theology to Theological Politics as Exemplified by Jürgen Moltmann and Stanley Hauerwas* (Lund: Lund University Press, 1994). Hauerwas later picked up this point himself: Stanley Hauerwas, *In Good Company: The Church as Polis* (Notre Dame, IN: University of Notre Dame Press, 1995).

11. Austin Farrer, *The End of Man* (London: SPCK, 1973), 52.

12. I here echo Lesslie Newbigin's understanding of the mission of the church: see Lesslie Newbigin, *A Word in Season: Perspectives on Christian Mission* (Grand Rapids: Eerdmans, 1994), 33.

13. Stanley Fish, *Is There a Text in This Class? The Authority of Interpretive Communities* (Cambridge, MA: Harvard University Press, 1980), 147–74.

14. Fish, *Is There a Text*, 141.

15. For the context of this phrase, see Rowan Williams, *Resurrection: Interpreting the Easter Gospel*, 2nd ed. (London: Darton, Longman & Todd, 2002), 61–62.

16. Charles Taylor, *Modern Social Imaginaries* (Durham, NC: Duke University Press, 2002), 23.

17. See here especially Alister E. McGrath, *Re-Imagining Nature: The Promise of Christian Natural Theology* (Oxford: Wiley-Blackwell, 2016).

18. William Whewell, *The Philosophy of the Inductive Sciences*, vol. 1 (London: Parker, 1847), 1.

19. N. R. Hanson, *Patterns of Discovery: An Inquiry into the Conceptual Foundations of Science* (Cambridge: Cambridge University Press, 1961).

20. Andrew Louth, "Theology, Contemplation, and the University," *Studia Theologica* 1, no. 2 (2003): 66.

21. Hare's personal reminiscences, as they touch on this theme, are instructive: Richard M. Hare, "A Philosophical Autobiography," *Utilitas* 14, no. 3 (2002): 269–305.

22. Iris Murdoch, "The Darkness of Practical Reason," in *Existentialists and Mystics*, ed. Peter Conradi (London: Chatto, 1998), 198.

23. I borrow this phrase from Kenneth Kirk's 1949 Charles Gore Memorial Foundation Lecture: see Kenneth E. Kirk, *The Coherence of Christian Doctrine* (London: SPCK, 1950), 1. Kirk attributes it to Charles Gore.

24. I here pick up on some key themes from the opening sections of Augustine's *de doctrina Christiana*, most notably the ideas of the *modus inveniendi* (discovering what is to be understood) and the *modus proferendi* (communicating what is to be understood).

25. For the important sociological notion of a "plausibility structure," see Peter L. Berger, *A Far Glory: The Quest for Faith in an Age of Credulity* (New York: Free Press, 1992), 125–26.

26. Gerhard Ebeling (1912–2001) is one of many theologians to point out how the Christian tradition enables a "new experience of experience." His protest against the "*Erfahrungsdefizit in der Theologie*" merits attention here: see Gerhard Ebeling, "Schrift und Erfahrung als Quelle theologischer Aussagen," *Zeitschrift für Theologie und Kirche* 75, no. 1 (1978): 99–116.

27. Rowan Williams, *On Christian Theology* (Oxford: Blackwell, 2000), 31.

28. For this approach in the parables of Jesus of Nazareth, see Marcus J. Borg, *Meeting Jesus Again for the First Time: The Historical Jesus and the Heart of Contemporary Faith* (San Francisco: HarperOne, 1994), 74.

29. Richard Dawkins, *A Devil's Chaplain: Selected Writings* (London: Weidenfeld & Nicholson, 2003), 19.

30. On this notion, see Ian James Kidd, "Receptivity to Mystery: Cultivation, Loss, and Scientism," *European Journal for Philosophy of Religion* 4, no. 3 (2012): 51–68.

31. This idea, as set out in Newman's *Grammar of Assent*, is helpfully explored in Anthony W. Keaty, "Newman's Account of the Real Apprehension of God: The Need for a Subjective Context," *Downside Review* 114, no. 394 (1996): 1–18.

Chapter 4 Books and the Discipleship of the Mind

1. Francis Bacon, *Aphorisms and Apothegms* (London: Scott, 1894), 204.

2. Marcel Proust, *La prisonnière* (Paris: Gallimard, 1925), 69; my translation.

3. C. S. Lewis, *An Experiment in Criticism* (Cambridge: Cambridge University Press, 1992), 137, 140–41.

4. C. S. Lewis, *Surprised by Joy* (London: HarperCollins, 2002), 249.

5. Lewis, *Surprised by Joy*, 221–22.

6. Bertrand Russell, *A History of Western Philosophy* (London: George Allen & Unwin, 1946), xiv.

7. C. S. Lewis, "On the Reading of Old Books," in *Essay Collection: Faith, Christianity and the Church*, ed. Lesley Walmsley (London: HarperCollins, 2002), 440.

8. T. S. Eliot, "Burnt Norton," in *Four Quartets* (Orlando: Harcourt, 1971), 14.

9. Lewis, *Surprised by Joy*, 197.

10. Neville Coghill, "The Approach to English," in *Light on C. S. Lewis*, ed. Jocelyn Gibb (London: Geoffrey Bles, 1965), 52.

11. Alister McGrath, *Emil Brunner: A Reappraisal* (Oxford: Wiley-Blackwell, 2016).

12. Pek van Andel and Danièle Bourcier, *De la serendipité dans la science, la technique, l'art et le droit: Leçons de l'inattendu* (Paris: Hermann, 2013), 293.

Chapter 5 The Balcony and the Road

1. William Temple, opening speech at the Second World Conference on Faith and Order, Edinburgh, 1937, available at https://nanopdf.com/download/william-temple-the-moravian-church_pdf#; quote at p. 4.

2. Søren Kierkegaard, *Concluding Unscientific Postscript*, trans. David F. Swenson (Princeton: Princeton University Press, 1941), 182.

3. John A. Mackay, *A Preface to Christian Theology* (London: Nisbet, 1941), 3. I apply Mackay's approach elsewhere in my works, such as Alister McGrath, *The Landscape of Faith: An Explorer's Guide to the Christian Faith* (London: SPCK, 2018), 42–44.

4. Mackay, *Preface to Christian Theology*, 20.

5. Mackay, *Preface to Christian Theology*, 29–54.

6. See, for example, John A. Mackay, *The Other Spanish Christ: A Study in the Spiritual History of Spain and South America* (New York: Macmillan, 1932). For a biography of Mackay, see John Mackay Metzger, *The Hand and the Road: The Life and Times of John A. Mackay* (Louisville: Westminster John Knox, 2010).

7. Mackay, *Preface to Christian Theology*, 29.

8. Mackay, *Preface to Christian Theology*, 30.

9. Mackay, *Preface to Christian Theology*, 30.

10. Mackay, *Preface to Christian Theology*, 45.

11. The title of the original version was "Suite du quatrième livre de l'Odyssée d'Homère ou les avantures de Télémaque fils d'Ulysse."

12. These are set out in C. A. Coulson, *Science and Christian Belief* (London: Oxford University Press, 1955), 97–102.

13. Abraham Pais, *J. Robert Oppenheimer: A Life* (Oxford: Oxford University Press, 2006), 90.

14. For my reflections on Coulson, see Alister McGrath, *Enriching Our Vision of Reality: Theology and the Natural Sciences in Dialogue* (London: SPCK, 2016), 27–41.

15. I have already noted Coulson, *Science and Christian Belief*. Two other works that I found very helpful were Charles A. Coulson, *Christianity in an Age of Science* (London: Oxford University Press, 1953), and Coulson, *Science and the Idea of God* (London: Epworth, 1960).

16. Mackay, *Preface to Christian Theology*, 183.

Chapter 6 The Creative Mind

1. Peter R. Dear, *The Intelligibility of Nature: How Science Makes Sense of the World* (Chicago: University of Chicago Press, 2008), 173.

2. Keith Yandell, *Philosophy of Religion: A Contemporary Introduction* (London: Routledge, 1999), 16.

3. Robert A. Emmons, *The Psychology of Ultimate Concerns: Motivation and Spirituality in Personality* (New York: Guilford Press, 1999).

4. Dariusz Krok, "The Role of Meaning in Life within the Relations of Religious Coping and Psychological Well-Being," *Journal of Religion and Health* 54, no. 6 (2015): 2292–308.

5. Alexander Wood, *In Pursuit of Truth: A Comparative Study in Science and Religion* (London: Student Christian Movement, 1927), 102.

6. Charles S. Peirce, *Collected Papers*, vol. 5, ed. Charles Hartshorne and Paul Weiss (Cambridge, MA: Harvard University Press, 1960), 172.

7. Daniel J. McKaughan, "From Ugly Duckling to Swan: C. S. Peirce, Abduction, and the Pursuit of Scientific Theories," *Transactions of the Charles S. Peirce Society* 44, no. 3 (2008): 446–68.

8. Gerhard Schurz, "Patterns of Abduction," *Synthese* 164, no. 2 (2008): 201–34, especially 205.

9. Claudio Rapezzi, Roberto Ferrari, and Angelo Branzi, "White Coats and Fingerprints: Diagnostic Reasoning in Medicine and Investigative Methods of Fictional Detectives," *British Medical Journal* 331 (2005): 1491–94.

10. Dorothy L. Sayers, *Les Origines du Roman Policier: A Wartime Wireless Talk to the French*, trans. Suzanne Bray (Hurstpierpoint, UK: Dorothy L. Sayers Society, 2003), 14.

11. William Whewell, *The Philosophy of the Inductive Sciences*, vol. 2 (London: John W. Parker, 1847), 36.

12. Dorothy L. Sayers, *The Unpleasantness at the Bellona Club* (London: Hodder & Stoughton, 1968), 155.

13. Sayers defends herself well on this point; see Dorothy L. Sayers, "Aristotle on Detective Fiction," *English: Journal of the English Association* 1, no. 1 (1936): 23–35.

14. Raymond Chandler, "The Simple Art of Murder," *Atlantic Monthly*, December 1944, 53–59.

15. Dorothy L. Sayers, *The Mind of the Maker* (London: Methuen, 1941), 145–74, especially 150–51.

16. Catherine M. Kenney, "*The Nine Tailors* and the Riddle of the Universe" and "*Gaudy Night* and the Mysteries of the Human Heart," in *The Remarkable Case of Dorothy L. Sayers* (Kent, OH: Kent State University Press, 1990), 53–80, 81–119.

17. Barbara Reynolds, ed., *The Letters of Dorothy L. Sayers: Child and Woman of Her Time* (Hurstpierpoint, UK: Dorothy L. Sayers Society, 2002), 97.

18. Sayers, *Mind of the Maker*, 171–73.

19. Sayers, *Mind of the Maker*, 15–24.

20. Sayers, *Mind of the Maker*, 172–73.

21. Ludwig Wittgenstein, *Notebooks, 1914–1916* (New York: Harper, 1961), 75.

22. See M. Neil Browne and Stuart M. Keeley, *Asking the Right Questions: A Guide to Critical Thinking*, 8th ed. (Upper Saddle River, NJ: Pearson Prentice Hall, 2007), 196.

23. See especially Robert J. Louden, *The World We Want: How and Why the Ideals of the Enlightenment Still Elude Us* (Oxford: Oxford University Press, 2007).

24. Dorothy L. Sayers, *Creed or Chaos?* (London: Methuen, 1947), 33.

25. Sayers, *Creed or Chaos?*, 24.

26. Sayers, *Mind of the Maker*, 25–36.

27. Sayers, *Mind of the Maker*, 97–99.

28. Dorothy L. Sayers, "Creative Mind," in *Unpopular Opinions* (New York: Harcourt, Brace, 1947), 49.

29. *The Practical Works of Richard Baxter*, vol. 13 (London: James Duncan, 1830), 29.

Chapter 7 C. S. Lewis on the Reasonableness of the Christian Faith

1. Rowan D. Williams, *The Lion's World: A Journey into the Heart of Narnia* (London: SPCK, 2012).

2. Donald Baillie, *St Andrews Citizen*, June 29, 1946, quoted in Walter Hooper, *C. S. Lewis: A Companion & Guide* (San Francisco: HarperSanFrancisco, 1996), 43–44.

3. For further details, see Alister E. McGrath, *C. S. Lewis—A Life: Eccentric Genius, Reluctant Prophet* (London: Hodder & Stoughton, 2013).

4. Lewis, *Surprised by Joy* (London: HarperCollins, 2002), 197.

5. Lewis, *Surprised by Joy*, 197.

6. Dante, *Paradiso*, canto 33, lines 55–56; my translation.

7. G. K. Chesterton, *The Everlasting Man* (San Francisco: Ignatius, 1993), 105.

8. Austin Farrer, "The Christian Apologist," in *Light on C. S. Lewis*, ed. Jocelyn Gibb (London: Geoffrey Bles, 1965), 37.

9. For the narrative, see C. S. Lewis, *The Voyage of the "Dawn Treader"* (London: HarperCollins, 1994), 91–92.

10. Lewis, *Surprised by Joy*, 267.

11. For a detailed discussion, see Alister E. McGrath, "A Gleam of Divine Truth: The Concept of Myth in Lewis's Thought," in *The Intellectual World of C. S. Lewis* (Oxford: Wiley-Blackwell, 2013), 55–82.

12. C. S. Lewis, "The Weight of Glory," in *Essay Collection: Faith, Christianity and the Church*, ed. Lesley Walmsley (London: HarperCollins, 2002), 98.

13. Lewis, "The Weight of Glory," 98.

14. Fiodore Dostoyevsky, "The Dream of a Ridiculous Man," in *A Disgraceful Affair: Stories*, trans. David Magarshack (London: Harper Perennial, 2009), 172.

15. Russell to Colette O'Niel, October 23, 1916, in *The Selected Letters of Bertrand Russell: The Public Years 1914–1970*, ed. Nicholas Griffin (London: Routledge, 2001), 85.

16. Katharine Tait, *My Father Bertrand Russell* (New York: Harcourt Brace Jovanovich, 1975), 189.

17. For what follows, see C. S. Lewis, *Mere Christianity* (London: HarperCollins, 2002), 135–36.

18. Lewis's apologetic method is often misunderstood. For a correction of earlier accounts of his approach, see Alister E. McGrath, "Reason, Experience, and Imagination: Lewis's Apologetic Method," in *The Intellectual World of C. S. Lewis*, 129–46.

19. C. S. Lewis, *The Four Loves* (London: HarperCollins, 2002), 25.

20. G. K. Chesterton, "The Return of the Angels," *Daily News*, March 14, 1903.

21. Lewis, *Mere Christianity*, 21.

22. C. S. Lewis, "Is Theology Poetry?," in *C. S. Lewis: Essay Collection and Other Short Pieces*, ed. Lesley Walmsley (London: Collins, 2000), 21.

Chapter 8 Listening and Engaging

1. The best study remains Timothy Dudley-Smith, *John Stott: A Biography*, 2 vols. (Leicester: Inter-Varsity, 1999).

2. John Stott, *Christian Mission in the Modern World* (Downers Grove, IL: InterVarsity, 2008).

3. I served as curate at St. Leonard's Church, Wollaton, Nottingham, from 1980 to 1983.

4. John Stott, *The Contemporary Christian: An Urgent Plea for Double Listening* (Leicester: Inter-Varsity, 1992), 13.

5. See, for example, the discussion of Gadamer's notion of *Horizontverschmelzung* (a "fusion of horizons") in the influential study of Anthony C. Thiselton, *The Two Horizons: New Testament Hermeneutics and Philosophical Description with Special Reference to Heidegger, Bultmann, Gadamer, and Wittgenstein* (Exeter: Paternoster, 1980). Stott knew this text well and referred to it often—for

example, in reflecting on the task of the preacher. See John R. W. Stott, *I Believe in Preaching* (London: Hodder & Stoughton, 1982), 137–38.

6. Stott, *Contemporary Christian*, 13.

7. Stott, *Christian Mission in the Modern World*, 285.

8. Stott, *Christian Mission in the Modern World*, 64–65.

9. I consider the issue of the significance of the identity of audiences for early Christian apologetics, looking closely at sermons in Acts directed toward Jews, Greeks, and Romans, in my four W. H. Griffith Thomas Lectures, given at Dallas Theological Seminary during February 1997. These were published as a series with the running title "Biblical Models for Apologetics" in *Bibliotheca Sacra* 155 (1998): 3–10, 131–38, 259–65, 387–93.

10. Stott, *Christian Mission in the Modern World*, 65–66.

11. Stott, *Christian Mission in the Modern World*, 10.

12. For my own reflections on this process of reflection, see Alister E. McGrath, *Iustitia Dei: A History of the Christian Doctrine of Justification*, 3rd ed. (Cambridge: Cambridge University Press, 2005).

13. For Stott's engagement with secularism, see Alister Chapman, "Secularisation and the Ministry of John R. W. Stott at All Souls, Langham Place, 1950–1970," *Journal of Ecclesiastical History* 56, no. 3 (2005): 496–513.

14. Stott, *Contemporary Christian*, 27–28.

15. Michael Ramsey, *Image Old and New* (London: SPCK, 1963), 14.

16. Stott, *Contemporary Christian*, 222.

17. Alister Chapman, *Godly Ambition: John Stott and the Evangelical Movement* (Oxford: Oxford University Press, 2012), 116.

18. John Stott, "Relevant Biblical Teaching: The Art of Double Listening," interview by Derek Morris, *Ministry* (January 1997): 8.

19. Chapman, *Godly Ambition*, 76.

20. John Stott, *Between Two Worlds: The Challenge of Preaching Today* (Grand Rapids: Eerdmans, 1982), 154.

21. Stott, *Christian Mission in the Modern World*, 67–68.

22. Stott, *Christian Mission in the Modern World*, 68.

23. Stott himself drew on this title in one of his finest works: John Stott, *The Incomparable Christ* (Leicester: Inter-Varsity, 2001). This work is based on Stott's four millennial lectures at All Souls, Langham Place.

24. See, for example, Alister McGrath, *The Landscape of Faith: An Explorer's Guide to the Christian Faith* (London: SPCK, 2018).

25. Emil Brunner, "Toward a Missionary Theology," *Christian Century* 66, no. 27 (1949): 816.

Chapter 9 J. I. Packer on Theology and Spirituality

1. Alister E. McGrath, *J. I. Packer: A Biography* (Grand Rapids: Baker, 1997).

2. Alister E. McGrath, *C. S. Lewis—A Life: Eccentric Genius, Reluctant Prophet* (London: Hodder & Stoughton, 2013); McGrath, *Emil Brunner: A Reappraisal* (Chichester: Wiley-Blackwell, 2014).

3. J. I. Packer, "Keswick and the Reformed Doctrine of Sanctification," review of Steven Barabas, *So Great Salvation: The History and Message of the Keswick Convention, The Evangelical Quarterly* 27 (1955): 167.

4. J. I. Packer, "The Comfort of Conservatism," in *Power Religion*, ed. Michael Horton (Chicago: Moody, 1992), 283–99.

5. J. I. Packer, "On from Orr: The Cultural Crisis, Rational Realism, and Incarnational Ontology," *Crux* 32, no. 3 (1996): 12–26. I personally regard this as one of Packer's finest pieces of writing.

6. J. I. Packer, *Truth and Power: The Place of Scripture in the Christian Life* (Wheaton: Harold Shaw, 1996), 117.

7. See further Alister McGrath, "Engaging the Great Tradition: Evangelical Theology and the Role of Tradition," in *Evangelical Futures: A Conversation on Theological Method*, ed. John G. Stackhouse (Grand Rapids: Baker Academic, 2000), 139–58.

8. C. S. Lewis, *An Experiment in Criticism* (Cambridge: Cambridge University Press, 1992), 137, 140–41.

9. J. I. Packer, "An Introduction to Systematic Spirituality," *Crux* 26 (1990): 6.

10. J. I. Packer, *Knowing God* (London: Hodder & Stoughton, 1975), 41.

11. J. I. Packer, interview with Amy Anderson, Regent College website, accessed May 23, 2018, http://www.regent-college.edu/about-us/news/2016/ji-packer -still-teaching-and-loving-it.

Chapter 10 Truth, Mystery, and Darkness

1. Locke to Mr. Molyneux, January 10, 1697–98 in *The Works of John Locke*, vol. 9, 11th ed. (London: Otridge and Son, 1812), 447.

2. John Locke, *An Essay concerning Human Understanding* in *Locke's Essays: An Essay concerning Human Understanding and a Treatise on the Conduct of Understanding* (Philadelphia: Hayes & Zell, 1854), 4.3.29, p. 376.

3. Alexander Pope, *Essay on Man*, 2nd ed., ed. Mark Pattison (Oxford: Clarendon, 1871), epistle 2, line 10, p. 37.

4. Pope, *Essay on Man*, epistle 2, line 1, p. 37.

5. Quoted in Richard Bernstein, "Once More Admired Than Bought, a Writer Finally Basks in Success," *New York Times*, May 15, 1990, http://www.nytimes .com/1990/05/15/books/once-more-admired-than-bought-a-writer-finally-basks -in-success.html. See further Brian McIlroy, "Pattern in Chaos: John Banville's Scientific Art," *Colby Quarterly* 31, no. 1 (1995): 74–80.

6. Werner Heisenberg, *Die Ordnung der Wirklichkeit* (Munich: Piper Verlag, 1989), 44; my translation.

7. Augustine, *Sermon* 117; my translation.

Chapter 11 Intelligibility and Coherence

1. Peter B. Medawar and Jean Medawar, *The Life Science: Current Ideas of Biology* (London: Wildwood House, 1977), 171.

2. José Ortega y Gasset, "El origen deportivo del estado," *Citius, Altius, Fortius* 9, no. 1–4 (1967): 259; my translation.

3. Ortega, "El origen deportivo del estado," 259–60.

4. C. S. Lewis, "Is Theology Poetry?," in *C. S. Lewis: Essay Collection and Other Short Pieces*, ed. Lesley Walmsley (London: HarperCollins, 2002), 21.

5. John Donne, *The First Anniversary: An Anatomy of the World*, line 213, in *The Epithalamions, Anniversaries, and Epicedes*, ed. W. Milgate (Oxford: Clarendon Press, 1978), 28.

6. Virginia Woolf, "A Sketch of the Past," in *Moments of Being*, ed. Jeanne Schulkind, 2nd ed. (New York: Harcourt Brace, 1985), 72.

7. Dante, *Paradiso*, canto 33, lines 85–90.

8. Hermann Hesse, "Die Sehnsucht unser Zeit nach einer Weltanschauung," *Uhu* 2 (1926): 3–14.

9. Nancy Cartwright, *The Dappled World: A Study of the Boundaries of Science* (Cambridge: Cambridge University Press, 1999).

10. C. S. Lewis, *Christian Reflections* (Grand Rapids: Eerdmans, 1967), 65.

11. John Keats, "Lamia," line 230, in *The Complete Poems*, Penguin Classics, 3rd ed. (London: Penguin, 1988), 431.

12. Mary Midgley, *The Myths We Live By* (London: Routledge, 2004), 39–40.

13. Mary Midgley, "Dover Beach," unpublished essay quoted in Nelson Rivera, *The Earth Is Our Home: Mary Midgley's Critique and Reconstruction of Evolution and Its Meanings* (Exeter: Imprint Academic, 2010), 179n21.

14. Mary Midgley, *Wisdom, Information, and Wonder: What Is Knowledge For?* (London: Routledge, 1995), 199.

15. As argued by Roy F. Baumeister, *Meanings of Life* (New York: Guilford, 1991).

16. Ursula Goodenough, *The Sacred Depths of Nature* (New York: Oxford University Press, 1998), 10.

17. Carl Sagan, *Pale Blue Dot: A Vision of the Human Future in Space* (London: Headline, 1995), vi.

Chapter 12 Hope in the Darkness

1. J. R. R. Tolkien, *The Return of the King* (London: George Allen & Unwin, 1966), 199.

Chapter 13 The Hope of Heaven

1. C. S. Lewis, "Is Theology Poetry?," in *C. S. Lewis: Essay Collection and Other Short Pieces*, ed. Lesley Walmsley (London: Collins, 2000), 21.

2. C. S. Lewis, *Mere Christianity* (London: HarperCollins, 2002), 134.

3. Lewis, *Mere Christianity*, 137.

4. C. S. Lewis, *The Last Battle* (New York: Collier, 1986), 162.

5. Lewis, *Last Battle*, 158.

6. Lewis, *Mere Christianity*, 137.

7. Lewis, *Mere Christianity*, 134.

Alister E. McGrath is the Andreas Idreos Professor of Science and Religion at Oxford University and director of the Ian Ramsey Centre for Science and Religion. He holds Oxford doctorates in the natural sciences, intellectual history, and Christian theology. McGrath has written extensively on the interaction of science and Christian theology and is the author of many books, including the international bestseller *The Dawkins Delusion? Atheist Fundamentalism and the Denial of the Divine* and the market-leading textbook *Christian Theology: An Introduction*.

Engage Skeptics with Intelligence and Imagination

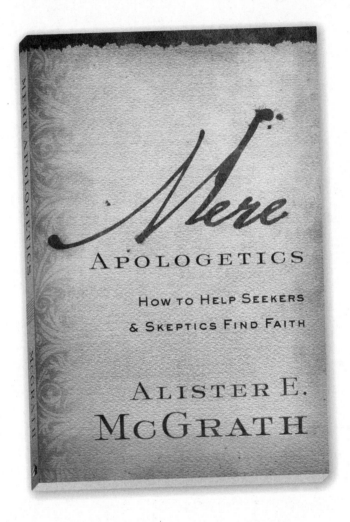

"This is a fresh, clear, and practical introduction to apologetics from someone who doesn't just talk about the subject but actually does it brilliantly."

—Os Guinness, author of *Long Journey Home*